SACRAMENTO PUBLIC LIBRARY

3 3029 04117 4418

COO          DEC 22 1999
BELLE COOLEDGE LIBRARY
5600 SOUTH LAND PARK DRIVE
SACRAMENTO, CA 95822

D1164669

imagine

# imagine

## The Spirit of 20th-Century American Heroes

EDITED AND COMPILED BY GINA MISIROGLU

NEW WORLD LIBRARY

NOVATO, CALIFORNIA

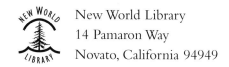

New World Library
14 Pamaron Way
Novato, California 94949

Copyright © 1999 by New World Library
Introduction © 1999 by Gina Misiroglu
Photo research managed by Gina Misiroglu
Cover design by Big Fish
Art direction and text design by Mary Ann Casler

All rights reserved. This book may not be reproduced in whole or in part, or transmitted in any form, without written permission from the publisher, except by a reviewer who may quote brief passages in a review; nor may any part of this book be reproduced, stored in a retrieval system, or transmitted in any form or by any means electronic, mechanical, photocopying, recording, or other, without written permission from the publisher.

Permission acknowledgments on page 117–118 are an extension of the copyright page. The editor has made every attempt to secure permission to reprint all excerpts, and cannot take responsibility for any errors or omissions. New World Library would be pleased to correct any errors in future editions of this book.

Library of Congress Cataloging-in-Publication Data

Imagine: the spirit of 20th-century American heroes / edited by Gina Misiroglu.
    p.    cm.
    Includes bibliographical references.
    ISBN 1-57731-086-1 (alk. paper)
    1. Speeches, addresses, etc., American.    2. United States — Civilization — 20th century Sources.    I. Misiroglu, Gina Renée.
PS661.I43    1999
815'.508 — dc21
                            99-30714
                               CIP

First Printing, October 1999
ISBN 1-57731-086-1

Printed in Korea on acid-free paper
Distributed to the trade by Publishers Group West

10 9 8 7 6 5 4 3 2 1

For Luke

We cannot live for ourselves alone. Our lives are connected by a thousand invisible threads,

and along these sympathetic fibers, our actions run as causes and return to us as results.

— *Herman Melville*

# Contents

imagine

# Introduction

The first transatlantic flight. Women's suffrage. The New Deal. The Cuban Missile Crisis. The civil rights march on Washington, D.C. Watergate. AIDS. During the twentieth century, Americans have experienced more distinct change per decade than perhaps any other nation. The human spirit has both soared and mourned as men and women of all creeds and colors redefined the nation, making us laugh, cry, and cheer over the changing times. These events, and the heroes that surround them, pay tribute in these pages to the terrain that is called twentieth-century America.

Embodying these major events, new expressions, and shifts in philosophy are the words that shape them. Whether speeches, writings, song lyrics, letters, or personal statements, a variety of mediums are used by leaders of all generations to effect change, garner support, or transform the ordinary into the sensational. Amelia Earhart, Gloria Steinem, Albert Einstein, Marian Wright Edelman, Muhammad Ali, Madeleine Albright, and John Lennon join a cast of leaders, artists, entertainers, builders, pioneers, scientists, thinkers, mavericks, and inspirational trailblazers who were the voices of a century. From the mouths of heroes as diverse as Fred Rogers and Dr. Martin Luther King Jr. these words — heartrending, tender, victorious, compassionate, motivational — challenge how we, as Americans, think.

Joseph Campbell, the great authority on heroes and myths, once said that the ultimate trial for a hero lies in losing him- or herself to a higher end. "When we quit thinking primarily about ourselves and our own self-preservation," Campbell said, "we undergo a truly heroic transformation of consciousness." Although this collection could not possibly represent all of the great men and women of this century, there are more than fifty expressions of heroism revealed here as a mosaic of perspectives, heritage, culture, and gender. The wealth of personal history and touching vignettes that have resulted from talks with and writings from these men and women pay testimony to their heroism and to how unique and yet universally true the American experience can be. As a celebration of wisdom and diversity, this glimpse of the times is meant to impart perspective: as participants we have only to look through these pages to recognize the milestones that have inextricably shaped us and our country.

As we begin a new century, it is apparent that something can be said of its effect on many generations of both natives and immigrants. The twentieth century has brought the United States to center stage; indeed, it has been called the American century. The results of modern technology and an ever-evolving popular culture are part of present-day America. Yet deep down we may not be all that different from our grandparents and great-grandparents. In all of its faces and philosophies, the American character may be one of the singular constants throughout history. *Imagine* celebrates the voices of the American character.

# Amelia Earhart

*"Everyone has his own Atlantics to fly. Whatever you want very much to do, against the opposition of tradition, neighborhood opinion, and so-called 'common sense' — that is an Atlantic."*

*With Charles Lindbergh's monumental 1927 flight to Paris, the world was smitten with aviation. Amelia Earhart, the first woman to fly solo across the Atlantic, continued the world's romance with flight. Although her historic flight was not the first time she had crossed the Atlantic — she had done that in June 1928, accompanied by two male pilots — it was the first time a woman had flown the Atlantic solo, and in record time. Subsequently, she performed a number of aviation firsts, many of which were also firsts for women. Her fame was almost instantaneous. With determination and outspokenness, Earhart became a colorful public figure, giving speeches and writing frequently and well — often about the future of aviation in the United States. Her theories on aviation in general, and on women in particular, echoed convincingly with audiences nationwide. The following guest editorial was written for a small aviation paper.*

One of the questions I am asked most frequently is what the future for women will be in aviation. Young girls who wish to study for aeronautical careers ask it, older women who wish to change their occupations, mothers who are thinking about their daughters' careers or those of the young men whom their daughters are planning to marry, and individuals who are interested for one reason or another in women's activities — all ask it.

Of course, my answer to the question is only my opinion. Aviation is an industry, and so far as I can see, there is no reason to suppose women's reaction to it will be different to their reaction to other industries. In the last twenty-five years, they have entered into hundreds of different businesses, and each year sees a surprising increase in the extent of their activities. Aviation is simply the fastest form of transportation, and will lure women as other forms have done. True, we do not see women driving autobuses, or locomotives, or being captains of steamships. But these occupations are only one phase of the transportation systems they represent, and hundreds of women are employed in each of them in other capacities. It may follow that women will never be pilots of passenger or mail planes on regular runs. However, they have opened up so many doors marked "Impossible" that I don't know where they'll stop. May I comment in passing that it is very difficult to say whether their disinclination to these so-called active jobs in general is due to inability or to inherited modes of thinking which the training of centuries has imposed. It seems to me until the same number of women are engaged in flying as men that there is absolutely no basis for comparison of abilities. At present in the United States there are fewer than a hundred women pilots of all grades and approximately eight thousand men.

From these figures it is sometimes implied that women have no influence upon aviation. From my contact with it I believe that view is erroneous. Women may not be actively engaged in it in so large numbers as men, and they may not be patronizing the airlines so frequently as men, but certainly their influence is being felt more and more strongly as commercial flying develops. . . .

As a [pilot] in the women's air derby from Santa Monica to Cleveland, I had an opportunity to see many interesting things. Not only did I have the privilege of knowing a large population of women flyers in this country, but I could study the reaction of other women who observed our comings and goings at control stops. A great proportion of the crowds which greeted us were women. They came out to see what their strange sisters looked like, and I believe when they saw how small and feminine some of the pilots were they changed their ideas of flying somewhat when they learned that most of the women in the race are earning their living by their connection in aeronautics.

. . . It is hard to draw a line between the influence that aviation has had on women and that which women have had on aviation. However, I am very sure that they are both important to each other and will become more closely allied as the industry realizes the value of their cooperation and women see how much aviation is trying to give them.

# A l b e r t   E i n s t e i n

*"God doesn't play dice with the world."*

*The creator of E=mc², German-born American physicist Albert Einstein radically transformed our understanding of the universe. An ardent humanist, he took an active and outspoken stand on political and social issues of his time. He philosophized on the meaning of life, love, God, and humanity, and was at the forefront of the campaign waged by atomic scientists in the mid-1940s to educate the world about the implications of nuclear energy and the necessity to halt nuclear weapon development. In 1955, Einstein worked with mathematician Bertrand Russell to reverse the cold war trend toward nuclear war, and one week before his death Einstein agreed to add his name to a manifesto urging all nations to give up nuclear weapons. The following is from Einstein's classic essay,* The World As I See It, *which describes his belief in humanity, a peaceful world, and the high mission of science.*

What an extraordinary situation is that of us mortals! Each of us is here for a brief sojourn; for what purpose he knows not, though sometimes he thinks he feels it. But from the point of view of daily life, without going deeper, we exist for our fellow men — in the first place for those on whose smiles and welfare all our happiness depends, and next for all those unknown to us personally with whose destinies we are bound up by the tie of sympathy. A hundred times every day I remind myself that my inner and outer life depend on the labors of other men, living and dead, and that I must exert myself in order to give in the same measure as I have received and am still receiving. I am strongly drawn to the simple life and am often repressed by the feeling that I am engrossing an unnecessary amount of labor of my fellow men. I regard class differences as contrary to justice and, in the last resort, based on force. I also consider that plain living is good for everybody.

In human freedom in the philosophical sense I am definitely a disbeliever. Everybody acts not only under external compulsion but also in accordance with inner necessity. Schopenhauer's saying, that "a man can do as he will, but not will as he will," has been an inspiration to me since my youth up, and a continual consolation and unfailing wellspring of patience in the face of the hardships of life, my own and others'. This feeling mercifully mitigates the sense of responsibility which so easily becomes paralyzing, and it prevents us from taking ourselves and other people too seriously; it conduces to a view of life in which humor, above all else, has its due place.

To inquire after the meaning or object of one's own existence or of creation generally has always seemed to me absurd from an objective point of view. And yet everybody has certain ideals which determine the direction of his endeavors and his judgments. In this sense I have never looked upon ease and happiness as ends in themselves — such an ethical basis I call more proper for a herd of swine. The ideals which have lighted me on my way and time after time given me courage to face life cheerfully, have been Truth, Goodness, and Beauty. Without the sense of fellowship with men of like mind, of preoccupation with the objective, the eternally unattainable in the field of art and scientific research, life would have seemed to me empty. The ordinary objects of human endeavor — property, outward success, luxury — have always seemed to me contemptible.

My passionate sense of social justice and social responsibility has always contrasted oddly with my pronounced freedom and the need for direct contact with other human beings and human communities. I gang my own gait and have never belonged to my country, my friends, or even my immediate family, with my whole heart; in the face of all these ties I have never lost an obstinate sense of detachment, or the need for solitude — a feeling which increases with the years. One is sharply conscious, yet without regret, of the limits to the possibility of mutual understanding and sympathy with one's fellow creatures. Such a person no doubt loses something in the way of geniality and light-heartedness; on the other hand he is largely independent of the opinions, habits, and judgments of his fellows and avoids the temptation to take his stand on such insecure foundations. . . .

The fairest thing we can experience is the mysterious. It is the fundamental emotion which stands at the cradle of true art and true science. He who knows it not and can no longer wonder, no longer feel amazement, is as good as dead, a snuffed-out candle. . . . A knowledge of the existence of something we cannot penetrate, of the manifestations of the profoundest reason and the most radiant beauty, which are only accessible to our reason in their most elementary forms — it is this knowledge and this emotion that constitute the truly religious attitude; in this sense, and in this alone, I am a deeply religious man.

# Lucille Ball

**1911–1989**

*"I never became truly confident until, in the Lucy character, I began to create something that was truly mine."*

*Lucille Ball's greatest legacy is the laughter that her memory continues to generate in her fans, both young and old alike. From the obscurity of a doubtful career as a New York model to top Hollywood stardom in motion pictures, radio, television, and theater, "Lucy," as she was affectionately known, entertained and endeared audiences the world over. Part raucous clown, part spirited muse, the determined, rebellious, and creatively illogical character of Lucy Ricardo, as portrayed in her 1950s hit, I Love Lucy, redefined comedy and became imbedded in the popular consciousness. Loved for its timeless wit, I Love Lucy is still the most popular show in the history of television. The First Woman of Television was a savvy businesswoman; when Ball bought out her co-owned (with husband Desi Arnaz) company Desilu Productions in 1962, she became the first woman president of a major Hollywood film production company. A piece she wrote in the 1980s shares the secrets of her success.*

When young performers ask me what is the key to success in show business, I assure them it is the same as in any other business. I can sum it up in two words — hard work. Luck, good and bad, plays a part in everyone's life, of course. And inborn talent for your chosen profession gives you an enormous advantage. But you still have to work hard.

By the time I was ready to go out into the world my family had taught me some wonderful philosophy — that you get back from this world what you put into it. Also, to never accept half values but to know what you want and then find a way to get it.

Certainly, there was nothing in the beginning to indicate I would be a success in show business. I didn't think I had much personality. I was retiring, I couldn't project, I didn't know how to walk across the floor. I got five jobs and lost them all. I even attended a drama school where the teacher told me, with the greatest of kindness, not to waste my money but to try some other profession.

But I was willing to do anything within reason to get into show business — sell tickets, change lightbulbs, sweep the floor, anything. And so I worked at it and I learned and eventually I became the Hattie Carnegie model and then a Goldwyn Girl. So the advice I give to youngsters trying to get ahead today is based on my own experience, not on theory.

Give yourself enough time to get to an appointment. If it takes thirty minutes, allow yourself thirty-five, not twenty-five, and then have to rush as most people do. Be known as a thinking employee. The smart young actress, for instance, not sure whether she'll be needed for a certain scene, has her hair and makeup ready just in case — and certainly knows her lines. Then, if the director asks if she can do the scene, she doesn't have to complain that she needs time to get ready. This is the kind of girl who makes it easy for directors and producers and they ask for her time and again.

Additionally, and most important, before you set short-range, overly ambitious goals about going to Hollywood to become an actor, prepare yourself first. Too many young people think they have talent, which they may well possess. But talent is not enough. It takes a lot of training and hard work to polish yourself into a competent performer.

You are much better off to achieve success on a local level before you venture out into a world that is already crowded with professionals. Get all the high school, college, and little theater experience you can at home until you have the confidence and ability that people will notice.

I have a theory which I call the art of selfishness; but it's a good selfishness. You put a sign on your mirror, asking, "Is it good for me?" Like staying out late, for instance; or letting yourself be talked into doing things you don't want to do; or being pulled apart by too many demands. When you permit people you love to depend on you too much you are actually hurting them as much as you are depriving yourself.

Perhaps you think that once you get to the top of your profession you can relax and take it easy. Not a chance. I don't have to sweep floors or change lightbulbs anymore, but if I started taking it easy, the quality of my work would decline, and you, the viewer, would soon notice it.

Like the head of any business firm, I work as hard today as I ever have. Perhaps harder.

# Muhammad Ali

*"Every day they die in Vietnam for nothing. I might as well stay right here and live or die for something."*

*Immediately after winning the heavyweight championship of the world in 1964, prize fighter Cassius Clay Jr. announced that he was a Black Muslim and had changed his name to Muhammad Ali. After defending the championship nine times within two years, Ali became one of the most controversial figures in American history. Two days before he refused to step into a U.S. Army induction center, the Olympic gold medalist stood behind a "freedom of religion" defense and confronted the nation with his principles: he was not going to Vietnam to "go fight in a war against people I don't know anything about." One hour after Ali refused induction, the New York State Athletic Commission suspended his boxing license and stripped him of his championship title. Ali regained his title in 1974 by knocking out George Foreman. In the early 1990s, Ali spoke to the two most important decisions he's ever made: defying the draft and changing his name.*

I never thought of myself as great when I refused to go into the army. All I did was stand up for what I believed. There were people who thought the war in Vietnam was right. And those people, if they went to war, acted just as brave as I did. There were people who tried to put me in jail. Some of them were hypocrites, but others did what they thought was proper and I can't condemn them for following their conscience either. People say I made a sacrifice, risking jail and my whole career. But God told Abraham to kill his son and Abraham was willing to do it, so why shouldn't I follow what I believed? Standing up for my religion made me happy; it wasn't a sacrifice. When people got drafted and sent to Vietnam and didn't understand what the killing was about and came home with one leg and couldn't get jobs, that was a sacrifice. But I believed in what I was doing, so no matter what the government did to me, it wasn't a loss.

Some people thought I was a hero. Some people said that what I did was wrong. But everything I did was according to my conscience. I wasn't trying to be a leader. I just wanted to be free. And I made a stand all people, not just black people, should have thought about making, because it wasn't just black people being drafted. The government had a system where the rich man's son went to college, and the poor man's son went to war. Then, after the rich man's son got out of college, he did other things to keep him out of the army until he was too old to be drafted. So what I did was for me, but it was the kind of decision everyone has to make. Freedom means being able to follow your religion, but it also means carrying the responsibility to choose between right and wrong. So when the time came for me to make up my mind about going in the army, I knew people were dying in Vietnam for nothing and I should live by what I thought was right. I wanted America to be America. And now the whole world knows that, so far as my own beliefs are concerned, I did what was right for me. . . .

Changing my name was one of the most important things that happened to me in my life. It freed me from the identity given to my family by slave masters. If Hitler changed the names of people he was killing, and instead of killing them made them slaves, after the war those people would have changed their slave names. That's all I was doing. People change their names all the time, and no one complains. Actors and actresses change their name. The pope changes his name. Joe Louis and Sugar Ray Robinson changed their names. If I changed my name from Cassius Clay to something like Smith or Jones because I wanted a name that white people thought was more American, nobody would have complained. I was honored that Elijah Muhammad gave me a truly beautiful name. "Muhammad" means one worthy of praise. "Ali" was the name of a great general [a cousin of the Prophet Muhammad and the third Caliphate after the death of the Prophet]. I've been Muhammad Ali now for twenty-six years. That's four years longer than I was Cassius Clay.

# Helen Keller

1880–1968

*"I try to make the light in others' eyes my sun, the music in others' ears my symphony, the smile on others' lips my happiness."*

*In April 1887, just a few weeks after Anne Sullivan was hired to teach the blind and deaf seven-year-old Helen Keller, the miracle occurred: the young girl associated water with the letters w-a-t-e-r that were spelled into her hand. From that day forward, Keller never stopped learning. A Radcliffe College graduate and the author of numerous books, including several autobiographies, Keller spent much of her life advocating for women's rights, pacifism, and the rights of the handicapped. She took a stand against World War I and supported controversial groups like the American Civil Liberties Union, the NAACP, and Margaret Sanger's birth control crusade. During World War II she brought inspiration to the bedsides of veterans who had lost their sight or hearing in battle, and fought to make Braille the standard printed communication for the blind. She lectured widely, and often spoke of the wonder and beauty of life. She wrote the following in the late 1920s.*

There is something divine in the art which some human beings possess to shape life for themselves, no matter what the outward circumstances may be. That is the power of the Celestial Artist, the Will, to find life worth living, despite the handicap imposed. I have for many years endeavored to make this vital truth clear; and still people marvel when I tell them that I am happy. They imagine that my limitations weigh heavily upon my spirit, and chain me to the rock of my despair. Yet, it seems to me, happiness has very little to do with the senses. If we make up our minds that this is a drab and purposeless universe, it will be that, and nothing else. On the other hand, if we believe that the earth is ours, and that the sun and moon hang in the sky for our delight, there will be joy upon the hills and gladness in the fields because the Artist in our souls glorifies creation. Surely, it gives dignity to life to believe that we are born into this world for noble ends, and that we have a higher destiny than can be accomplished within the narrow limits of this physical life.

"I can understand," I hear someone interrupting me, "that you enjoy flowers and sunshine and that sort of thing, but when you sit by yourself in that little study on the top of the house all day, aren't you dreadfully bored? You can't see a bit of color from your window, or hear a sound! Aren't the days and the hours all alike to you?" Never! My days are all different, and no hour is quite like another.

Through my sense of touch I am keenly alive to all changes and movements of the atmosphere, and I am sure the days carry for me as much as they do for my friend who observes the skies — often not caring about their beauty, but only to see if it is going to rain. There are days when the sun pours into my study, and I feel all of life's joys crowded into each beam. There are rainy days when a sort of shade clings about me and lays a cool hand upon my face, and the smell of the moist earth and damp objects lingers everywhere. . . . There is the hour when the morning sun kisses me awake, and the hour when the burden of material things drops from my shoulder, and I drift to Slumberland. There are hours of breathless haste to catch up with the letters that cover my desk, hours of glad expectancy when a beautiful dream seems about to come true, hours fragrant with tender memories; and always there are the endless varied hours I spend with the thinkers and poets and philosophers of all times! How can there be a full moment when my books are all about me! . . .

Limitations drive one inward for diversion, with the result that one's own thoughts become absorbingly interesting. The small events of daily life take on extraordinary importance when the Celestial Artist combines them with the spiritual elements in the laboratory of mind. It is a miracle how an incident of no particular value comes out of the mental crucible beautiful and precious. Little by little the transformation and classification of ideas take place in the brain, where are registered the beings and the events which give delight to circumscribed lives. Stored in the memory, they furnish plentiful entertainment for solitary hours; and that is why I never feel "deaf blind." I left that horrible abyss of hopelessness long, long ago.

# Jackie Robinson

*"I was a martyred hero to a lot of people who seemed to have sympathy for the underdog."*

*Jackie Robinson became the first African-American baseball player in the major leagues when he was brought up as an infielder for the Brooklyn Dodgers in 1947. His indomitable spirit and "smoldering rancor" spurred him through difficult early years with the Dodgers when he was a frequent target of racial slurs from peers and fans alike. Ultimately he became "the second most popular American" (behind Bing Crosby, in a nationwide poll) and led the Dodgers to six National League championships and their first-ever World Series victory in 1955. After abruptly retiring from baseball the cantankerous Robinson spoke out on behalf of civil rights and social injustices — supporting Dr. Martin Luther King Jr. and campaigning for presidential candidate Richard Nixon "in a last-ditch battle to keep the Republicans from becoming completely white." Despite his impact on America's favorite pastime and his influence in social and political arenas, Robinson believed he really "never had it made."*

I guess if I could choose one of the most important moments in my life, I would go back to 1947, in the Yankee Stadium in New York City. It was the opening day of the World Series and I was for the first time playing in the series as a member of the Brooklyn Dodgers team. It was a history-making day. It would be the first time that a black man would be allowed to participate in a world series. I had become the first black player in the major leagues.

I was proud of that and yet I was uneasy. I was proud to be in the hurricane eye of a significant break-through and to be used to prove that a sport can't be called national if blacks are barred from it. Branch Rickey, the president of the Brooklyn Dodgers, had rudely awakened America. He was a man with high ideals, and he was also a shrewd businessman. Mr. Rickey had shocked some of his fellow baseball tycoons and angered others by deciding to smash the unwritten law that kept blacks out of the big leagues. He had chosen me as the person to lead the way.

It hadn't been easy. Some of my own teammates refused to accept me because I was black. I had been forced to live with snubs and rebuffs and rejections. Within the club, Mr. Rickey had put down rebellion by letting my teammates know that anyone who didn't want to accept me could leave. But the problems within the Dodgers club had been minor compared to the opposition outside. It hadn't been that easy to fight the resentment expressed by players on other teams, by the team owners, or by bigoted fans screaming "nigger." The hate mail piled up. There were threats against me and my family and even out-and-out attempts at physical harm to me.

Some things counterbalanced the ugliness. Black people supported me with total loyalty. They supported me morally; they came to sit in a hostile audience in unprecedented numbers to make the turnstiles hum as they never had before at ballparks all over the nation. Money is America's God, and business people can dig black power if it coincides with green power, so these fans were important to the success of Mr. Rickey's "Noble Experiment." . . .

In a very real sense, black people helped make the experiment succeed. Many who came to the ballpark had not been baseball fans before I began to play in the big leagues. Suppressed and repressed for so many years, they needed a victorious black man as a symbol. It would help them believe in themselves. But black support of the first black man in the majors was a complicated matter. The breakthrough created as much danger as it did hope. It was one thing for me out there on the playing field to be able to keep my cool in the face of insults. But it was another for all those black people sitting in the stands to keep from overreacting when they sensed a racial slur or an unjust decision. . . .

There I was the black grandson of a slave, the son of a black sharecropper, part of a historic occasion, a symbolic hero to my people. The air was sparkling. . . . It should have been a glorious moment for me as the stirring words of the national anthem poured from the stands. Perhaps it was, but then again perhaps the anthem could be called the theme song for a drama called The Noble Experiment. Today as I look back on the opening game of my world series, I must tell you that it was Mr. Rickey's drama and that I was only a principal actor. As I write this twenty years later, I cannot sing the anthem. I cannot salute the flag; I know that I am a black man in a white world. In 1972, in 1947, at my birth in 1919, I know that I never had it made.

# Rachel Carson

**1907–1964**

*"Future generations are unlikely to condone our lack of prudent concern for the integrity of the natural world that supports all life."*

*Many call marine biologist Rachel Carson the mother of the modern environmental movement. Learning that her friend's bird sanctuary was destroyed by the pesticide DDT sprayed under a state mosquito control program, she vowed to speak out "or there would be no peace for me." In 1962, her passion for the natural world and years of research on the effects of pesticides culminated in the publication of her most influential — and controversial — work,* Silent Spring, *a detailed exposé of the injurious effects of chemical pesticides on the environment, especially DDT. Violently attacked by the agricultural chemical industry, the book led to a presidential commission that endorsed her findings, triggering legislation banning the use of DDT. Although Carson's work ignited an environmental consciousness unprecedented in the United States, her words of bold challenge are perhaps more relevant today than forty years ago. The following is from* Silent Spring.

The history of life on earth has been a history of interaction between living things and their surroundings. To a large extent, the physical form and the habits of the earth's vegetation and its animal life have been molded by the environment. Considering the whole span of earthly time, the opposite effect, in which life actually modifies its surroundings, has been relatively slight. Only within the moment of time represented by the present century has one species — man — acquired significant power to alter the nature of his world.

During the past quarter century this power has not only increased to one of disturbing magnitude but it has changed in character. The most alarming of all man's assaults upon the environment is the contamination of air, earth, rivers, and sea with dangerous and even lethal materials. This pollution is for the most part irrecoverable; the chain of evil it initiates not only in the world that must support life but in living tissues is for the most part irreversible. In this now universal contamination of the environment, chemicals are the sinister and little-recognized partners of radiation in changing the very nature of the world — the very nature of its life. Stronium 90, released through nuclear explosions into the air, comes to earth in rain or drifts down as fallout, lodges in soil, enters into the grass or corn or wheat grown there, and in time takes up its abode in the bones of a human being, there to remain until his death. Similarly, chemicals sprayed on croplands or forests or gardens lie long in soil, entering into living organisms, passing from one to another in a chain of poisoning and death. Or they pass mysteriously by underground streams until they emerge and, through the alchemy of air and sunlight, combine into new forms that kill vegetation, sicken cattle, and work unknown harm on those who drink from once pure wells. As Albert Schweitzer has said, "Man can hardly even recognize the devils of his own creation."

It took hundreds of millions of years to produce the life that now inhabits the earth — eons of time in which that developing and evolving and diversifying life reached a state of adjustment and balance with its surroundings. The environment, rigorously shaping and directing the life it supported, contained elements that were hostile as well as supporting. Certain rocks gave out dangerous radiation; even within the light of the sun, from which all life draws its energy, there were shortwave radiations with power to injure. Given time — time not in years but in millennia — life adjusts, and a balance has been reached. For time is the essential ingredient; but in the modern world there is no time. . . .

Along with the possibility of the extinction of mankind by nuclear war, the central problem of our age has therefore become the contamination of man's total environment with such substances of incredible potential for harm — substances that accumulate in the tissues of plants and animals and even penetrate the germ cells to shatter or alter the very material of heredity upon which the shape of the future depends.

# John Lennon

*"We all have Hitler in us, but we also have love and peace. So why not give peace a chance for once?"*

*When "Imagine" was released in 1971, the title track to the album was a welcome reprieve from postwar machinations of the past decades, and quickly enchanted the world with its existential call for universal altruism. The album established pop star, composer, songwriter, and ex-Beatle John Lennon's credibility as a performer in his own right outside the auspices of the Fab Four. After his marriage to Japanese artist Yoko Ono, Lennon and his partner campaigned ardently for world peace, introducing nontraditional peace campaign tactics such as Bagism and releasing titles like "Give Peace a Chance," which became the national anthem for pacifists across the nation. "Imagine" is probably the most widely revered of all Lennon's songs: its Utopian dream and melodic musings are praised for their appeal to both the secular and more spiritually minded.*

Imagine there's no heaven,
It's easy if you try,
No hell below us,
Above us only sky,
Imagine all the people
Living for today . . .

Imagine there's no countries,
It isn't hard to do,
Nothing to kill or die for,
No religion too,
Imagine all the people
Living life in peace . . .

Imagine no possessions,
I wonder if you can,
No need for greed or hunger,
A brotherhood of man,
Imagine all the people
Sharing all the world . . .

You may say I'm a dreamer,
But I'm not the only one,
I hope some day you'll join us,
And the world will live as one.

# Martha Graham

*"I don't think about what I have done; I only think of the things that I want to do, and haven't done."*

*Often called a temperamental genius, Martha Graham is the diva of twentieth-century dance. Dancing and choreographing well into her seventies, Graham created a totally new form of dance expression, an interpretive free-form movement that became known as the Graham technique. By redefining dance as both art and the most basic form of human expression, she gave direction to the modern dance movement and created a methodology of movement and vocabulary that is taught the world over. She founded the Martha Graham Dance Company, the oldest continuously performing company in America, in which she remained the sole artistic creator until her death. The Martha Graham School of Contemporary Dance continues to train students in the Graham technique. For Graham, the essence of dance was "the expression of man, the landscape of his soul." It is in this spirit that she briefly touched on her philosophy of movement.*

I am a dancer.

I believe that we learn by practice. Whether it means to learn to dance by practicing dancing or to learn to live by practicing living, the principles are the same. In each it is the performance of a dedicated precise set of acts, physical or intellectual, from which comes shape of achievement, a sense of one's being, a satisfaction with spirit. One becomes in some area an athlete of God.

To practice means to perform, in the face of all obstacles, some act of vision, of faith, of desire. Practice is a means of inviting the perfection desired.

I think the reason dance has held such an ageless magic for the world is that it has been the symbol of the performance of living. Even as I write, time has begun to make today yesterday — the past. The most brilliant scientific discoveries will in time change and perhaps grow obsolete, as new scientific manifestations emerge. But art is eternal, for it reveals the inner landscape, which is the soul of man.

Many times I hear the phrase "the dance of life." It is an expression that touches me deeply, for the instrument through which the dance speaks is also the instrument through which life is lived — the human body. It is the instrument by which all the primaries of life are made manifest. It holds in its memory all matters of life and death and love. Dancing appears glamorous, easy, delightful. But the path to the paradise of the achievement is not easier than any other. There is fatigue so great that the body cries, even in its sleep. There are times of complete frustration, there are daily small deaths. Then I need all the comfort that practice has stored in my memory, a tenacity of faith.

It takes about ten years to make a mature dancer. The training is twofold. First comes the study and practice of the craft which is the school where you are working in order to strengthen the muscular structure of the body. The body is shaped, disciplined, honored, and in time, trusted. The movement becomes clean, precise, eloquent, truthful. Movement never lies. It is a barometer telling the state of the soul's weather to all who can read it. This might be called the law of the dancer's life — the law which governs its outer aspects.

Then comes the cultivation of the being from which whatever you have to say comes. It doesn't just come out of nowhere, it comes out of a great curiosity. The main thing, of course, always is the fact that there is only one of you in the world, just one, and if that is not fulfilled then something has been lost. Ambition is not enough; necessity is everything. It is through this that the legends of the soul's journey are retold with all their tragedy and their bitterness and sweetness of living. It is at this point that the sweep of life catches up with the mere personality of the performer, and while the individual becomes greater, the personal becomes less personal. And there is grace. I mean the grace resulting from faith . . . faith in life, in love, in people, in the act of dancing. All this is necessary to any performance in life which is magnetic, powerful, rich in meaning.

# James Dean

*"Dream as if you'll live forever, live as if you'll die today."*

*James Dean had one of the most remarkably brief careers of any screen star. Although he made only three films, in little over a year Dean became a national personality, a personification of the restless American youth of the mid-1950s he portrayed in the classic film* Rebel Without a Cause. *In September 1955, just a few months shy of two of his films —* Rebel Without a Cause *and* Giant *— hitting the box office, Dean was killed in a car accident. Nominated for two Academy Awards for his performances in* East of Eden *and* Giant, *Dean, as articulated by biographer Joe Hymans, "had the intuitive talent for expressing the hopes and fears that are a part of all young people . . . [and] managed to dramatize brilliantly the questions every young person in every generation must resolve." Although Dean mused much about life, he held the craft of acting in high regard, and spoke candidly in many interviews about his first love.*

An actor must interpret life, and in order to do so must be willing to accept all the experiences life has to offer. In fact, he must seek out more of life than life puts at his feet. In the short span of his lifetime, an actor must learn all that there is to know, experience all there is to experience, or approach that state as close as possible. He must be superhuman in his efforts to store away in the core of his subconscious everything that he might be called upon to use in the expression of his art. . . .

To grasp the full significance of life is the actor's duty; to interpret it is his problem; and to express it is his dedication. Being an actor is the loneliest thing in the world. You are all alone with your concentration and your imagination, and that's all you have. Being a good actor isn't easy. Being a man is even harder. I want to be both before I'm done. . . .

When an actor plays a scene exactly the way a director orders, it isn't acting. It's following instructions. Anyone with the physical qualifications can do that. So the director's task is just that — to direct, to point the way. Then the actor takes over. And he must be allowed the space, the freedom, to express himself in the role. Without that space, an actor is no more than an unthinking robot with a chestful of push buttons. . . .

It was an accident, although I've been involved in some kind of theatrical function or other since I was a child — in school, music, athletics. To me, acting is the most logical way for people's neuroses to manifest themselves, in this great need we have to express ourselves. To my way of thinking, an actor's course is set even before he's out of the cradle. . . .

There is always somebody in your life who opens your eyes and makes you see your mistakes and stimulates you to the point of trying to find your way. Not of rectifying your mistakes, but of growing. In my life, that somebody was James Whitmore. He encouraged me to go to New York and with the fortification of his knowledge of theater and the right way of working, I went. Whitmore was working for Warner's when I came out [to Hollywood], and I wanted to thank him for his kindness and patience, but he said, "It's not necessary. Elia Kazan did the same thing for me, and you will do the same for somebody else." I feel that I have been of some benefit to young actors. It's the only way to repay Jimmy.

# Hillary Clinton

**b. 1947**

*"Women have been on the front lines in the battle for human rights and individual dignity for a very long time. But we are finally hearing their voices."*

*Having survived Whitewater, the health care reform blunder, impeachment, the president's possible indictment, and nation- wide embarrassment, First Lady Hillary Clinton lends new meaning to the tired cliché, grace under fire. Touting themes of universal health care, equal pay for women, affordable child care, and gun control, Clinton unapologetically balances her roles of dedicated wife, mother, advocate, author, and humani- tarian. As Clinton's future role in politics looks bright, the American public recognizes the First Lady not just as a veteran of perhaps the most celebrated sex scandal in history, but the perpetual force behind her husband — instituting the tax credit for stay-at-home moms, initiating the $50 million in grants to help children on Medicaid treat their asthma, and advocating for increased funds to train pediatricians in children's hospitals. The following is from a speech Ms. Clinton presented on United Nations International Women's Day, 1999.*

Many women around the world are finding their voice in new ways. And as we stand here together we have to do all that we can to make sure that those voices are amplified, their stories are heard and told.... One single story can pierce through and make it clear that we are all in the same story, we all face the same challenges: What lessons will we bring from this twentieth century into the twenty-first? How will we honor the past? But look at it with very open eyes, recognizing the tragedy, the violence, the hor- ror that has beset this century, but also appreciating the advances, the scientific discoveries, the new ways that women and men have been able to create new lives and opportunities.

One of the most powerful lessons we have learned . . . is that a nation's progress depends not only on pro- tecting women's fundamental human rights, but on ensuring that those women have access to what we call the tools of opportunity. No nation, with all respect, can expect to succeed in the global economy of the twenty- first century if half of its people lack the opportunity and the right to make the most of their God-given poten- tial. Now that does not mean that there is only one way that that potential can be realized. There are as many different life paths for women as there are for men. In fact, I would argue, perhaps even more because of our obligations and desires to have and raise children, our commitment to relationships both close at home and further outside our families. But what we must strive for is to create the conditions in which women have the right to make the choices in their lives for themselves. . . . No nation can hope to move forward if its women and children are trapped in endless cycles of poverty; when they don't have the health care they need; when too many of them still die in childbirth; when they cannot read or take a job for which they will receive equal pay for equal work. . . .

It was in preparation for [the president's] trip to China that I first heard that wonderful saying that, "Women hold up half the sky." It's a powerful image of what women do every single day, in every country, as we struggle to raise families, pass on our values, and participate fully in the life of our communities. . . .

As we move toward this twenty-first century, let us acknowledge that women cannot hold up half the sky if they are robbed of the education they deserve to have and denied the right to go to school. They cannot hold up half the sky if they don't have access to the credit, the loans, and the jobs they need to lift themselves and their families out of poverty. They cannot hold up half the sky if they are victims of abuse in their own homes, or kidnapped and become objects of war or sold into marriage, slavery, or other disastrous life circumstances. Women cannot hold up half the sky if they are denied the freedom to plan their own families, if they are denied their basic legal rights. Women can only hold up half the sky . . . if their feet are planted firmly on the soil of freedom and equal justice.

My hope is that into the next century we will not only continue to see progress, but advancements in every part of the world. We will see a world in which all citizens — men and women — enjoy the freedoms of lib- erty; in which all children are valued and given equal opportunities whether they are boys or girls; and in which every citizen can live in dignity, free from fear, and filled with hope. Only then will we be able to say — with honesty — that, yes, women not only can but do hold up half the sky. And that sky over all of us is filled with a bright future for our boys and, especially, our girls.

# Jim Henson

*"Inside, we're all children. Everybody identifies with that feeling of looking around at this big world and not knowing who you are and what you're supposed to be doing here."*

*In the 1960s, television pro-ducer Joan Ganz Cooney began work on a children's educational TV show called Sesame Street. She asked emerging puppeteer Jim Henson to create a family of characters to populate the show, which resulted in the characters we have all come to love: Ernie and Bert, Oscar the Grouch, Grover, Cookie Monster, and Big Bird. Unaware of his empire-in-the-making, Henson began work on* The Muppet Show, *where characters like Miss Piggy and Kermit the Frog charmed their way into our hearts. Innovator, popular artist, and performing genius, Jim Henson sought to stretch the envelope of modern technology with his award-winning animatronic work and imaginative vision for what could be possible on screen — and garnered kudos for his versatility and marketing savvy. That he brought delight and wonder to audiences worldwide is secondary only to the love he showed for children and the special character-audience bond he fostered.*

Over the years, I've evolved my own set of beliefs and attitudes — as we all have — that I feel works for me. I don't feel particularly comfortable telling other people how to think or live. There are people who know much more about these things than I do, but here goes. . . .

I believe that life is basically a process of growth — that we go through many lives, choosing those situations and problems that we will learn through. I believe that we form our own lives, that we create our own reality, and that everything works out for the best. I know I drive some people crazy with what seems to be ridiculous optimism, but it has always worked out for me.

I believe in taking a positive attitude toward the world, toward people, and toward my work. I think I'm here for a purpose. I think it's likely that we all are, but I'm only sure about myself. I try to tune myself in to whatever it is that I'm supposed to be, and I try to think of myself as a part of all of us — all mankind and all life. I find it's not easy to keep these lofty thoughts in mind as the day goes by, but it certainly helps me a great deal to start out this way.

I love my work, and because I enjoy it, it doesn't really feel like work. Thus I spend most of my time working. I like working collaboratively with people. At its best, the film and television world functions creatively this way. I have a terrific group of people who work with me, and I think of the work that we do as "our" work.

I don't know exactly where ideas come from, but when I'm working well ideas just appear. I've heard other people say similar things — so it's one of the ways I know there's help and guidance out there. It's just a matter of our figuring out how to receive the ideas or information that's there waiting to be heard.

I find that it's very important for me to stop every now and then and get recharged and reinspired. The beauty of nature has been one of the great inspirations in my life. Growing up as an artist, I've always been in awe of the incredible beauty of every last bit of design in nature. The wonderful color schemes of nature, which always work harmoniously, are particularly dazzling to me. I love to lie in an open field looking up at the sky. One of my happiest moments of inspiration came to me many years ago as I lay on the grass, looking up into the leaves and branches of a big old tree in California. I remember feeling very much a part of everything and everyone.

Working as I do with the movement of puppet creatures, I'm always struck by the feebleness of our efforts to achieve naturalistic movement. Just looking at the incredible movement of a lizard or a bird, or even the smallest insect, can be a very humbling experience.

At some point in my life I decided, rightly or wrongly, that there are many situations in this life that I can't do much about — acts of terrorism, feelings of nationalistic prejudice, cold war, etc. — so what I should do is concentrate on the situations that my energy can affect.

I believe that we can use television and film to be an influence for good; that we can help to shape the thoughts of children and adults in a positive way. As it has turned out, I'm very proud of some of the work we've done, and I think we can do many more good things.

When I was young, my ambition was to be one of the people who made a difference in this world. My hope still is to leave the world a little bit better for my having been here.

It's a wonderful life and I love it.

# Margaret Bourke-White

1906–1971

*"Photography is a window on the world."*

*In 1929, when* Time *editor Henry R. Luce was laying plans for a new magazine called* Fortune, *he hired industrial photographer Margaret Bourke-White. Her assignments ranged from coverage of the major industries of the United States to the rural poverty of American sharecroppers and tenant farmers. Her creation of the photo essay inaugurated the premiere issue of* Life *and set the tone for the magazine's visual force. As the first accredited woman photographer of World War II, she soon became the first woman photojournalist of American history, and her frontline images from twenty-eight countries brought the American public London during the Blitz, World War II battles, Joseph Stalin and the Kremlin, and the liberation of India and Pakistan. Over the course of her thirty-year career "Maggie" risked her life countless times for the perfect shot; she often recalled her encounter with Mahatma Gandhi, whom she photographed just six hours before he was assassinated.*

It's a little hard for me to talk about photography as a leisure-time pursuit. I don't take pictures for fun, although I have great fun taking pictures. My hobby was not photography, but natural science. When I went to college I was fully determined to make biology my life work. But I had the good fortune to be broke, and so turned to photography to make my way.

Photography has a strange way of taking you by the hand and leading you places you never dreamed you were going. I am sure the amateur has noticed this, and certainly those of us who are in the business of photojournalism are aware of this. In my own case, my camera has sent me to such places as the North Magnetic Pole, to the upper air eight miles high above Kansas in a jet plane, into the deepest gold mines in the world two miles straight down under Johannesburg, and more recently into the jungles of Honduras riding on the back of a mule. . . .

My camera — or should I say cameras — because if you're a photographer you accumulate cameras like barnacles — have been the means of bringing me within focusing distance of such widely different personalities as General Patton and Pope Pius, the White Queen of Bechuanaland, Winston Churchill, President Roosevelt, President Eisenhower, and the emperor of Japan. While all this is fun, it carries responsibility with it. I think all of us who are in this profession of photojournalism accept very seriously our obligation to be true interpreters of the twentieth century.

The photographer who goes out in search of these pictures of contemporary events and personages participates to an extraordinary degree, and often has to do some odd things in a day's work, as when I first photographed Mahatma Gandhi. Like many busy men, Gandhi had five secretaries. When I reached the most authoritative of these, I explained to the secretary that I had come to photograph the Mahatma at a spinning wheel.

"Do you know how to spin?" asked the secretary.

"I didn't come to spin with Gandhi. I came to photograph him spinning."

"How can you hope to understand the soul of the Mahatma at his spinning wheel," said the secretary, "unless you first master the principles of spinning?"

It was useless for me to protest I had a deadline to meet. Before I could photograph Gandhi I had to submit to a lesson in spinning. I was awkward at it and kept breaking the thread. To cover my embarrassment, I tried to joke about it. "Photography and spinning — they're both handicrafts."

"But the greater of the two," said the secretary, "is spinning." . . .

After a while, Gandhi's secretary informed me that I was going to witness a demonstration on Gandhi's personal spinning wheel. This was to be the climax of my instruction. I waited breathlessly to see how the Indians did the trick. But, as the demonstrator gave the wooden wheel its first turn, my faith in the machine age was suddenly justified. Gandhi's spinning wheel fell apart — folded flat as an accordion. After that, I heard no more about the deep symbolism of spinning and was about to take my pictures in peace. . . .

More perhaps than the correspondent, who works with words and may sometimes depend on interviews to report an event, the photographer must be there, must be participating in the march of history to an extraordinary degree. . . . Sometimes, I come away from what I have been photographing sick at heart, with the faces of people in pain etched as sharply in my mind as on my negatives. But I must go back because I feel it is my place to take such pictures.

# J o n a s   S a l k

*"I recognized the importance and value of . . . empathetically shifting perspective in dealing with human problems as well as in unraveling the mysteries of nature."*

*Dr. Jonas Salk developed the now-famous Salk vaccine for polio, claiming "personal responsibility" for his discovery by testing the drug on himself and his children before releasing it for widespread use. With mass inoculations in effect in 1954, Salk achieved the conquest of America's most deadly disease, reducing the incidence of polio by as much as 95 percent and preventing hundreds of thousands of cases in the United States. Salk received no royalties from the sale of his vaccine, was nominated for a Nobel Prize but didn't win it, and was never invited to join the National Academy of Sciences. In fact, many argued that his research was "applied science," and that competitive vaccines would deem Salk's obsolete. Salk turned his attention to cancer research and world peace. The following perspective, published in his* Anatomy of Reality *more than fifteen years ago, places Salk as one of the scientific greats.*

I do not remember exactly at what point I began to apply this way of examining my experience, but very early in my life I would imagine myself in the position of the object in which I was interested. Later, when I became a scientist, I would picture myself as a virus, or a cancer cell, for example, and try to sense what it would be like to be either. I would also imagine myself as the immune system, and I would try to reconstruct what I would do as an immune system engaged in combating a virus or cancer cell.

When I had played through a series of such scenarios on a particular problem and had acquired new insights, I would design laboratory experiments accordingly. I soon found myself in a dialogue with nature using viruses, immune systems, and other phenomena to ask questions in the form of experiments and then waiting for the answer. Based upon the results of the experiment, I would then know what questions to ask next, until I learned what I wanted to know, or until I went as far as I could go. When I observed phenomena in the laboratory that I did not understand, I would also ask questions as if interrogating myself: "Why would I do that if I were a virus or a cancer cell, or the immune system?" Before long, this internal dialogue became second nature to me; I found that my mind worked this way all the time.

When I started to ask larger questions about the human world, it came naturally to me to play the same kind of game. I soon found myself shifting my perspective, as I did in relation to my scientific work, from that of the participating subject to that of the objective observer. When I began to look at myself and at conditions of human life, I sought a perspective from outside myself and outside the "here and now," as well as from within. I needed a different, broader perspective. . . .

I realized that I had discovered a useful way to understand what was happening in the world and to examine its relationship to nature — to the evolutionary process, and to the human mind. I was able to imagine myself outside these phenomena as well as in them, in the same way as I had been able to imagine myself inside or outside a virus, or a cell, or an immune system. I began to imagine what might be done to ameliorate or improve the human condition, just as I had tried to imagine what could be done to destroy the infectivity of a virus without removing its capacity to immunize; what I would do to stimulate the immune system against a disease without the organism having to go through the experience of the infection itself. . . .

This experience underlined, in a very striking way, the value of being able to look at any event in life from more than one perspective. Being able to see things and to see oneself only from one point of view entailed limitations. When I had had the experience of seeing from many different points of view, I could see and feel so much more; I then discovered what the words identification and empathy meant. I could identify with a virus or a cell or with the immune system; I could also empathize with people in different situations, circumstances, and states of mind. I realized that, objectively speaking, there was not one fixed point of view or one perspective, but many changing points of view that depended upon varying circumstances. This revealed to me the value of participation as well as of suppleness and flexibility in my own perspective as an observer. I developed the capacity to shift my perspectives. . . . I then imagined that it may be possible, through empathy and intention, to influence the future course of human events in the same way that we can influence the course of human events through the use of the scientific and artistic imagination.

# Grandma Moses

*"If I didn't start painting, I would have raised chickens. I could still do it now."*

*Anna Mary Robertson Moses was an enterprising farmer's wife, whose tenacity developed a butter concern, opened a potato-chip business, and ran a family farm. Largely self-taught, she began to paint rural scenes for pleasure when she was in her seventies. Art collector Louis Calder spotted her work in a drugstore window, and it wasn't long until she became a name in the New York art scene. Perhaps the icon of American folk art, Moses is embraced for her charmingly naive style and her ability to bring alive the rural scenes and activities of a simpler, now nonexistent period of American life. A symbol for fruitful old age, Moses witnessed two world wars, and the advent of the automobile, airplane, and countless other inventions — much of which she never commented on. She continued to paint well into her one hundredth year, often mentioning it as the one thing that gave her real pleasure, but never once acknowledging her gift as heroic.*

In my mother's day, if a woman could write her own name, that was all that was necessary. When my mother was seven years old, she commenced to go to school and she left school when she was eleven, then she went into housework and from there she got married and when she was twenty-one she had three babies. That way of living was a kind of education. . . .

It is hard in this age for one to realize how we grew up at all. I felt older when I was sixteen than I ever did since. I was old and sedate when I left the Whitesides, I suppose it was the life I led, I had to be so ladylike. Even now I am not old, I never think of it, yet I am a grandmother to eleven grandchildren, I also have seventeen great-grandchildren, that's a plenty!

Things have changed greatly and still are changing, can they change much more? Can you think of any more improvements? My father liked his fireplace the same as I like my old iron stove, and now they have gas and electric ranges, but I would not be surprised, when the younger generation gets old, when people of coming generations, a hundred years from now, will look back upon us as primitives.

And yet I wonder sometimes whether we are progressing. In my childhood days life was different, in many ways, we were slower, still we had a good and happy life, I think, people enjoyed life more in their way, at least they seemed to be happier, they don't take time to be happy nowadays. But when you come to big questions like that, don't think too much, you must skip them, same as I did when I read the Bible to earn my silver thimble!

I have written my life in small sketches, a little today, a little yesterday, as I thought of it, as I remembered all the things from childhood and through the years, good ones and unpleasant ones, that is how they come, and that is how we have to take them. I look back on my life like a good day's work, it was done and I feel satisfied with it. I was happy and contented, I knew nothing better and made the best out of what life offered. And life is what we make it, always has been, always will be.

# Billy Graham

b. 1918

*"I believe the fundamental crisis of our time is a crisis of the spirit."*

*Perhaps America's most respected and admired evangelical leader of the past half-century, Billy Graham has achieved a lifetime of outreach unparalleled in human history. His crusades have reached over 100 million people, and well over 2 billion people worldwide have been touched by his television ministry. More than an evangelist, Dr. Graham is also a champion of human rights. In the 1950s, he personally removed the dividing ropes between whites and blacks at crusades in the then-segregated South. In the 1970s, he traveled to South Africa and called apartheid a sin. In the 1980s, he journeyed behind the still closed Iron Curtain to encourage victims of religious persecution. His recent efforts include the establishment of the Ruth and Billy Graham Children's Health Center for chronically ill children in the Appalachian Mountains. Upon receiving the Congressional Gold Medal as a great civic leader of the twentieth century, Dr. Graham looked forward to the new millennium with a message for America.*

Exactly 218 years ago, on May 2, 1778, the first recipient of this award, George Washington, issued a general order to the American people. He said: "The . . . instances of providential goodness which we have experienced and which have now almost crowned our labors with complete success demand from us . . . the warmest returns of gratitude and piety to the Supreme Author of all Good."

We are standing at a similar point in our history as less than four years from now the world will enter a new millennium. What will it hold for us? Will it be a new era of unprecedented peace and prosperity? Or will it be a continuation of our descent into new depths of crime, oppression, sexual immorality, and evil?

Ironically, many people heralded the dawn of the twentieth century with optimism. The steady march of scientific and social progress was going to bring a Christian era to this century. They believed that it would vanquish our social and economic problems. Some optimistic theologians even predicted the twentieth century would be "The Christian Century," as humanity followed Jesus' exhortation to love your neighbor as yourself. But no other century has been ravaged by such devastating wars, genocides, and tyrannies.

Our mood on the brink of the twenty-first century is much more somber. Terms like "ethnic cleansing," "random violence," and "suicide bombing" are now part of our daily vocabulary.

You know the problems as well as I do: racial and ethnic tensions that threaten to rip apart our cities and neighborhoods; crime and violence of epidemic proportions in most of our cities; children taking weapons to school; broken families; poverty; drugs; teenage pregnancy; corruption. The list is almost endless. . . .

Almost three thousand years ago, King David, the greatest king Israel ever had, sat under the stars and contemplated the reasons for the human dilemma. In Psalm 23, he touched on the three greatest problems of the human race. First, David said, is the problem of emptiness. . . . Second, is the problem of guilt. . . . Third, is the problem of death. . . . These three things — emptiness, guilt, and the fear of death — haunt our souls.

But we must probe deeper. Why is the human heart this way? The reason is because we are alienated from our Maker. That was the answer David found to these three problems. I believe the fundamental crisis of our time is a crisis of the spirit. It is not simply social and educational. We have lost sight of the moral and spiritual principles on which this nation was established — principles drawn largely from the Judeo-Christian tradition, as found in the Bible. . . .

We must commit our lives to God, and to the moral and spiritual truths that have made this nation great. Think how different our nation would be if we sought to follow the simple yet profound injunctions of the Ten Commandments and the Sermon on the Mount. But we must respond to God, who is offering us forgiveness, mercy and supernatural help, and the power to change. Our commitment must be translated into action — in our homes, in our neighborhoods, and in our society. Jesus taught that there are only two roads in life. There's the broad road that is easy and well traveled, but which leads to destruction. The other, He said, is the narrow road of truth and faith that at times is hard and lonely, but which leads to life and salvation.

As we face the new millennium, I believe America has gone a long way down the wrong road. We must turn around and go back, and change roads. If we ever needed God's help, it is now. If we ever needed spiritual renewal, it is now. And it can begin today in each of our lives, as we repent before God and yield ourselves to Him and His Word.

# Madeleine Albright

b. 1937

*"I draw encouragement especially from the memory of women who have dared to stand up and fight for human dignity and freedom."*

*Madeleine Korbel Albright became the first female secretary of state and the highest ranking woman in the United States government in 1997 after a unanimous confirmation by the Senate. Both in her current position and as a former U.S. representative to the United Nations, Albright has focused her mission on creating policies to help guide the world into a new century of peace, primarily through concentration on a bipartisan approach to foreign policy. Her accomplishments include the ratification of the Chemical Weapons Convention and steps toward stability in Eastern Europe. As a refugee whose family fled Czechoslovakia, first from the Nazis and later from the Communists, Albright represents the success of visionary immigrants. An advocate for international humanitarianism, Albright spoke of America's role in the post–cold war world in her remarks at the Carnegie Endowment for International Peace in Washington in 1998.*

What matters most for the future of our children is not the preoccupations of the moment, but whether the broad opportunities of this era are squandered or seized. For example, will the trends towards open markets and free trade grind to a halt as a result of the financial crisis? Will the worldwide movements toward democracy continue or go into reverse? Will we succeed in curbing the spread of weapons of mass destruction, or find ourselves confronted in the new century with catastrophes unmatched even by those of old? And will we find a way to resolve conflicts and build a global culture of peace, or be surrounded by regional and civil wars conducted with ever-more deadly weapons at ever-greater risks to our own society?

These are the questions that matter. But perhaps above all is a question related to each of the others: Will the United States of America continue to lead, or will we hide our heads in the sand out of indifference, complacency, or fear? Will we, in years to come, play the role of eagle, or ostrich?

Some suggest that Americans have turned inward and are not willing to bear the costs and risks of leadership. I don't believe that, but I do know that we have reached a critical moment in our effort to shape the post–cold war world. Now, more than ever, we need bipartisan support in Congress and broad support from the American people. Because only with that will we succeed in our broad objective of bringing the world closer together around basic principles of democracy, open markets, law, and a commitment to peace. . . .

A half-century ago our nation was in the midst of a bitterly bipartisan election campaign as candidates fought for the levers of political power. But in that same testing year of 1948, a Democratic president and a Republican Congress approved the Marshall Plan, laid the groundwork for NATO, established the Voice of America, recognized the infant state of Israel, airlifted life-sustaining aid to a blockaded Berlin, and helped an embattled Turkey and Greece remain on freedom's side of the Iron Curtain.

There are those who say that Americans have changed and that we are now too inward-looking and complacent to shoulder comparable burdens. But by standing tall, and backing our leadership with resources, we have the opportunity to prove the cynics wrong.

American foreign policy is not the province of a particular party, ideology, or point of view. It finds strength not in its brilliance of theory, but in the steadfast qualities of the American people — whose interests it defends and whose values it reflects. Through this century we have survived and prevailed against aggression, depression, fascism, and the totalitarian threat. Now, we face new dangers and uncertainties. But we have not lost our confidence, nor have we grown weary. For our country, there are no final frontiers. We are doers. Whatever threats the future may hold, we will meet them. With the memory alive in our hearts of past sacrifice, we will defend our freedom, meet our responsibilities, and live up to our principles.

# Babe Didrikson Zaharias

*"My goal was to be the greatest athlete that ever lived."*

*Babe Didrikson Zaharias is crowned by sports aficionados the female athletic phenomenon of this century. Her unabashed pursuit of athletic excellence forever changed the face of women's sports, and her perpetual optimism encouraged fellow athletes and fans alike. Although she mastered tennis and basketball, excelled in organized baseball, and received two gold medals for track and field in the 1932 Olympics, the majority of her career was dedicated to her accomplishments in golf. A maverick player before there were pro golf tours for women, she achieved seventeen straight major tournament victories in 1946 and 1947, including the U.S. Women's Amateur and the British Women's Amateur. The latter achievement made her the first American to win the British title. She was a three-time winner of the Women's National [Golf] Open, and a founding member of the Ladies' Professional Golf Association. Diagnosed with cancer in 1953, Babe continued to play golf. She expressed this sentiment shortly after her diagnosis.*

Once we had the doctor's diagnosis, nobody made a secret of the fact that I had cancer. I've never understood why cancer should be unmentionable. In golf, you know where the sand traps and water holes are ahead and you try to guide your shots accordingly. With cancer, you know that recovery will require something more than surgical skill, so — in a sort of spiritual way — you guide your shots.

Soon the newspapers everywhere announced that I had cancer. Thousands of cancer patients and thousands of others who were afraid of the disease wrote, wired, and telephoned in the few days before my operation.

Everybody promised prayers.

This was something new for me. All my life, I looked upon prayer as something very personal between God and me. I guess I've prayed for the same blessings and with the same gratitude as everyone else, but it never occurred to me that thousands of people, separated from each other, could effectively join in a barrage of prayers for the sake of one person — for me.

Being an athlete, I could express my feelings by saying: "Here is wonderful teamwork in faith."

Many times after a tournament, I recalled, a fan would say something like, "My heart was in my mouth when you lined up that tricky putt on the tenth hole. I was praying all the time." Yet I didn't think anybody was really praying. Now, lying in the hospital, waiting for surgery, I felt differently. If I was going to be all right again, I'd need more than my own prayers: I'd need the ones of everyone who had promised them.

Suddenly I looked upon prayers as muscles, and I realized that the strongest people in the world must be those who pray for each other. There was strength in this sharing, but I soon realized that I had to give to others as well as accept for myself. It would help us all move closer to God, "from Whom all blessings flow." Praying for each other struck me as spiritual training which kept everyone spiritually fit to deserve those blessings.

After the operation, the doctor came to me. "All right, Babe," he said, "I want to see you up and out of here real soon, and before the season's over I want to read on the sports pages that you've won another tournament." . . .

Suddenly I realized that golf now for me was more than a sport. Because of what it would symbolize to thousands of cancer patients — a victory through spiritual strength — my game would become, in a way, a symbol of faith.

# Franklin D. Roosevelt

*"The only thing we have to fear is fear itself."*

*Assuming the presidency at the depth of the Great Depression, Franklin D. Roosevelt took the reins of a nation faced with its greatest crisis since the stock market crash of 1929. In an effort to banish "the fear of the present and the future which held the American people and the American spirit in its grasp," Roosevelt initiated his New Deal — putting thousands to work for the government and setting up alphabet agencies to infuse the nation's economy. By imposing controls over banks and public utilities and establishing the Works Projects Administration and the Social Security Act, Roosevelt refurbished America until the beginnings of World War II. Roosevelt sought neutrality legislation to keep the United States out of the war, and created the United Nations under his vision for world peace. The only president to be elected for third and fourth terms, Roosevelt made four inaugural speeches; his second confidently outlines the continuation of New Deal programs.*

I am justified in believing that the greatest change we have witnessed has been the change in the moral climate of America. Among men of good will, science and democracy together offer an ever-richer life and ever-larger satisfaction to the individual. With this change in our moral climate and our rediscovered ability to improve our economic order, we have set our feet upon the road of enduring progress.

Shall we pause now and turn our back upon the road that lies ahead? Shall we call this the promised land? Or, shall we continue on our way? For "each age is a dream that is dying, or one that is coming to birth." Many voices are heard as we face a great decision. Comfort says, "Tarry a while." Opportunism says, "This is a good spot." Timidity asks, "How difficult is the road ahead?"

True, we have come far from the days of stagnation and despair. Vitality has been preserved. Courage and confidence have been restored. Mental and moral horizons have been extended. But our present gains were won under the pressure of more than ordinary circumstances. Advance became imperative under the goad of fear and suffering. The times were on the side of progress.

To hold to progress today, however, is more difficult. Dulled conscience, irresponsibility, and ruthless self-interest already reappear. Such symptoms of prosperity may become portents of disaster! Prosperity already tests the persistence of our progressive purpose. Let us ask again: Have we reached the goal of our vision of that fourth day of March 1933? Have we found our happy valley?

I see a great nation, upon a great continent, blessed with a great wealth of natural resources. Its 130 million people are at peace among themselves; they are making their country a good neighbor among the nations. I see a United States which can demonstrate that, under democratic methods of government, national wealth can be translated into a spreading volume of human comforts hitherto unknown, and the lowest standard of living can be raised far above the level of mere subsistence. But here is the challenge to our democracy: In this nation I see tens of millions of its citizens — a substantial part of its whole population — who at this very moment are denied the greater part of what the very lowest standards of today call the necessities of life.

I see millions of families trying to live on incomes so meager that the pall of family disaster hangs over them day by day.

I see millions whose daily lives in city and on farm continue under conditions labeled indecent by a so-called polite society half a century ago.

I see millions denied education, recreation, and the opportunity to better their lot and the lot of their children.

I see millions lacking the means to buy the products of farm and factory and by their poverty denying work and productiveness to many other millions.

I see one-third of a nation ill-housed, ill-clad, ill-nourished.

It is not in despair that I paint you that picture. I paint it for you in hope — because the Nation, seeing and understanding the injustice in it, proposes to paint it out. We are determined to make every American citizen the subject of his country's interest and concern; and we will never regard any faithful law-abiding group within our borders as superfluous. The test of our progress is not whether we add more to the abundance of those who have much; it is whether we provide enough for those who have too little.

If I know aught of the spirit and purpose of our Nation, we will not listen to Comfort, Opportunism, and Timidity. We will carry on.

# Maya Lin

b. 1960

*"I'm really interested in a nation's memory and how art really deals with a country's conscience."*

*Architect and sculptor Maya Lin created the most visited public American artwork of the twentieth century, the National Vietnam Veterans Memorial. Then a twenty-one-year-old architecture major at Yale University, Lin answered the call to create a monument to the U.S. military as part of a nationwide competition sponsored by the Vietnam Veterans Memorial Fund. Known as The Wall, Lin's design consists of two long, straight panels of black granite that, sloping beneath ground level to rest at an angle, bear the names of the 58,000 men and women who were killed in the Vietnam war or missing in action. Lin herself defines the work as "a journey," a process of grief and contemplation through which visitors travel. Dedicated in 1982, the memorial generated controversy for its simplistic design, and Lin was forced to defend it at public hearings in Washington. Lin continues to create public artworks around the country, and discusses the challenges of her work as independent artist.*

I think the difference between art and architecture can be compared to the difference between poetry and prose. For me the parallel to sculpture would be poetry, where every part of whatever you make has to be of perfect pitch and, for me at least, completely intuited and immediate. Whereas in writing a novel . . . every sentence you make must be grammatically correct, just the way you have to choose every single doorknob and latch and piece of furniture inside a residential house. I won't say that one is easier than the other — they are extremely different and I'm fascinated by those differences. . . .

I think I've always felt my work should be quite sensitive, not just site specific. In the very beginning with the *Vietnam Veterans Memorial*, one of the issues at hand was to make a work that would not demolish or hurt the trees that were already there. They thought I was actually a bit strange when I asked them to relocate a couple of trees and to maintain the park. I asked the landscape architect who had designed Constitutional Gardens to come back in and be my landscape architect on the project so that there would be continuity with that landscape. I think I've always tried to not fight nature, so whatever I might do is not combative but additive, so that I'm working with the environment. . . .

Time is something that has always been a part of the public works as chronologies. It brings you into a notion of real time and real experience so that anyone can read it and put themselves back in that place or become part of the real time of the piece. The *Women's Table* graphically and truthfully tells of the growth and emergence of women at Yale, which, in a way, chronicles the emergence of women in modern times. The spiral itself was also chosen specifically to make a beginning but leave the future completely open — unlike, say, the *Vietnam Veterans Memorial*, where the beginning and end of the war meet at the apex. The names start on the right-hand side, go around always clockwise, ending up back at the apex on the bottom of the left with '75. That one has a very finite time period, it's a closed circle. . . .

I think I've always made the studio sculptures at the same time I've been making the large outdoor pieces. One can't exist without the other, though I've been somewhat shy or hesitant to let these studio sculptures out. It's also because of the way architecture is set up. Architecture tends to grab all of your time. . . . There are actually two different dichotomies going on within the work. One is the public/private aspect, in which even my early public work carried some essential aspects of my private sculpture. The other one is just emerging as my first houses get built — I am really beginning to see a split between pure architecture and sculpture. I work simultaneously, yet separately, as sculptor and architect.

I was fortunate enough to have worked on the two main emotional events of the 1960s, of my childhood. In a way I think I absorbed all that when I was a child and these monuments are what came out: I think of it as unbiased. And I retired from memorial making at that point and am really not interested in doing more of them. I think I was interested in those because of their political nature, not necessarily the funereal aspects of them. I continue to believe that it is important for each one of us to give back to our world, our communities, in whatever way we can. I tried to do this when dealing with the Vietnam War, the civil rights movement, and issues of equality. . . . At this point I see myself very happily pursuing architecture and sculpture. . . . I absolutely cherish the differences between the two fields.

# Charlie Chaplin

*"Life is a tragedy when seen in close up, but a comedy in long shot."*

*Charlie Chaplin and his Little Tramp character rose to fame in 1915 — as Chaplin wooed movie audiences with his vaudevillian slapstick comedy for only a nickel. Although America's King of Comedy reached unprecedented fame during the silent picture era as a writer, director, and star, it was his controversial 1940 film* The Great Dictator *that broke true creative barriers. Abandoning his signature pantomime technique in order to play two speaking parts, Adolf Hitler and a little Jewish barber, Chaplin presented his antifascist beliefs to a neutral-standing America whom he urged to enter the war against the Nazis. Although the film was a huge success and garnered a bouquet of Academy Award nominations, it labeled Chaplin a communist sympathizer and ultimately led to his being barred from the United States. In the film, during an identity mix-up, the little barber is mistakenly introduced as "the future emperor of the world" and announces he does not wish to be emperor. He delivers the following speech.*

I'm sorry but I don't want to be an emperor; that's not my business. I don't want to rule or conquer anyone. I should like to help everyone, if possible. Jew, gentile, black, white. We all want to help one another; human beings are like that. We want to live by each other's happiness, not by each other's misery. We don't want to hate and despise one another. In this world, there's room for everyone and the good world is rich and can provide for everyone. The way of life can be free and beautiful. But we have lost the way. Greed has poisoned men's souls, has barricaded the world with hate, has goose-stepped us into misery and bloodshed. We have developed speed but we have shut ourselves in. Machinery that gives abundance has left us in want. Our knowledge has made us cynical; our cleverness, hard and unkind. We think too much and feel too little. More than machinery, we need humanity. More than cleverness, we need kindness and gentleness. Without these qualities, life will be violent, and all will be lost. The airplane and the radio have brought us closer together; the very nature of these inventions cries out for the goodness in men. Cries out for universal brotherhood, for the unity of us all. Even now my voice is reaching millions throughout the world — millions of despairing men, women, and little children; victims of a system that makes men torture and imprison innocent people. To those who can hear me, I say, "Do not despair." The misery that is now upon us is but the passing of greed, the bitterness of men who fear the way of human progress. The hate of men will pass and dictators die. And the power they took from the people will return to the people. And so long as men die, liberty will never perish.

Soldiers, don't give yourself to brutes. Men who despise you, enslave you, who regiment your lives, tell you what to do, what to think, and what to feel. Who drill you, diet you, treat you like cattle, use you as cannon fodder. Don't give yourselves to these unnatural men. Machine men with machine minds and machine hearts! You are not machines, you are not cattle, you are men! You have the love of humanity in your hearts — you don't hate. Only the unloved hate. The unloved and the unnatural! Soldiers, don't fight for slavery! Fight for liberty! In the seventeenth chapter of St. Luke it is written: The kingdom of God is in man. Not one man, nor a group of men, but in all men. In you — you the people have the power. The power to create machines, the power to create happiness. You the people have the power to make this life free and beautiful, to make this life a wonderful adventure!

Then, in the name of democracy, let us use that power! Let us all unite! Let us fight for a new world. A decent world that will give man a chance to work, that will give you the future and old age of security. By the promise of these things, brutes have risen to power. But they lie. They do not fulfill that promise. They never will. Dictators free themselves, but they enslave the people. Now let us fight to fulfill that promise! Let us fight to free the world! To do away with greed, with hate and intolerance. Let us fight for a world of reason, a world where science and progress lead to all men's happiness.

Soldiers! In the name of democracy, let us all unite!

Hannah? Can you hear me? Wherever you are? Look up, Hannah. The clouds are lifting. The sun is breaking through. We are coming out of the darkness into the light. We are coming into a new world, a kind new world. Where men will rise above their hate, their greed and brutality. Look up, Hannah, the soul of man has been given wings! And at last he is beginning to fly. He is flying into the rainbow, into the light of hope, into the future — the glorious future that belongs to you, to me, and to all others. Look up Hannah . . . Look up. . . .

# Maggie Kuhn

*"Speak your mind — even if your voice shakes, well-aimed slingshots can topple giants."*

At the age of sixty-five, after being forced to retire from her career as an educator and social action leader in the Presbyterian Church, Maggie Kuhn founded the Gray Panthers, a nonprofit group uniting young and old to eradicate ageism in the United States and bring about social justice. Kuhn defined "ageism" before the concept made its way into the public consciousness, and quickly gained attention as the popular spokesperson for an organization of international impact, literally jump-starting a contemporary cultural revolution. The Gray Panthers now has more than forty-five chapters across the country, and consultative status at the United Nations. Dispelling the myth that aging is synonymous with adjectives like decrepid, weak, or powerless, Kuhn spoke "outrageously" on behalf of older citizens, and her keynote address at the Conference of Conscious Aging in 1992 embodies her mission to change "the issue of aging and the images of aging."

Dr. Robert Butler, in his book *Why Survive? Being Old in America*, cites six myths that are widely held about old age. The first is that old age is a disease, a loathsome disease. You never admit how old you are, or, my goodness, you get a face-lift if you can. It's a disease. I say it's a triumph — a triumph over loss, failure, sadness, frustration, and rage. . . . The second is that old age is mindless. It's just a question of time before your brains get soft. Senility is inevitable. Nothing could be further from the truth. . . . Contemplate the number, the large numbers, of older people who are going to college today and working for masters and doctorates, and [are] exceedingly prolific as scholars — in late life. Learning never stops till rigor mortis sets in.

The third myth is that old age is sexless. "It's not appropriate for you, grandma; you can't do it anymore." Well, I say that until the end some form of intimacy and loving relationship is necessary. . . . The fourth myth is that old age is useless. "They don't do that anymore, you know." But I say that the skills and the experience and the survival opportunities that we present are prized possessions in the changing world. Without historical perspective, there is no future!

The fifth myth is that old age is powerless. It is true that many of us have infirmities. I have osteoporosis, I have arthritis, I have macular degeneration in both eyes, but I still have a head, and my head still works. And I have a memory and historical perspective that my peers share, and that historical perspective is extraordinarily important for the future. It cannot be denied. And the sixth myth is that all old people are alike. We are all cranky and crotchety and hard to get along with. And I say: For contrast, think of Ronald Reagan and me. . . . .

I'd like to remind you that the process of aging begins with birth. . . . One of my one-liners is that it begins with conception and ends in resurrection. You get the point? It's lifelong. The process of aging doesn't begin when you first find a wrinkle or another gray hair. The process of aging we share with all living creatures — all the plants, all the birds, all the reptiles, all the animals, including the human animal. And what we have done in an ageist society, in a society that sets old age apart, is to violate the essential wholeness and continuity of life — which is so, so regrettable. . . .

In order to survive and strive, you need a goal and a purpose — a passionate purpose that you do everything in your power to work for. . . . One [of my goals] is to celebrate our ethnicity, to understand and reach out to those who are different in race and ethnic and religious background from mine. But we are part of a human family. We are one race, and we celebrate it. And this to me represents a long spiritual journey to understand the oneness that transcends diversity and strife and hatred and fear. And it brings life together in wholeness and joy and peace. I am very concerned about the fact that so many of my peers do not have a goal. You retire from a job, and you retire from life. Right? The rocking chair and the leisure world. What a waste! We who have no risk to fear, we who have historical perspective, [should] be leading the change; [we should] be out of the rocking chairs. No more rocking chairs! No more leisure worlds!

# Neil Armstrong

**b. 1930**

*"That's one small step for a man, one giant leap for mankind."*

*Neil Armstrong will always be remembered as the first man to walk on the moon. On July 20, 1969, as a worldwide television audience tracked the historic flight of* Apollo 11, *Armstrong stepped down from the lunar module* Eagle *onto the Sea of Tranquility, dug the first handful of lunar soil, and collected the first moon rocks. Following* Apollo 11 *Armstrong served at NASA Headquarters in Washington, and became known as an advocate of research in computer control of high-performance aircraft. His was an early voice urging the United States to create a permanently manned space station. An intensely private person, Armstrong refrained from making public appearances, but was catapulted back into the spotlight when he was named head of the committee investigating the* Challenger *explosion in 1986. In one of his earlier public appearances, on the first anniversary of* Apollo 11's *historic flight, Armstrong reminisced about his historic feat and the meaning of space travel in this century.*

I see the moon from the back yard as a friendly place. And I see a lot of landmarks. I can no longer just look at it just as a spot in the sky; but, rather, I actually pick out, of course, the Sea of Tranquility, Clavius, Aristarchus, and places I know and have flown by, just as a traveler when looking at a globe picks out particular spots because they have particular memories to him, and he remembers events that happened at that point. And I do the same. . . .

I remember the elation of finding out that we indeed weren't going to sink into the surface and we could continue with all other planned activities. The first step was the most important from that point of view; not the point of view that it was the first step, but, rather, from the point of view that it proved that we could continue with all the other things we had hoped to do. I certainly can remember a large number of other individual things that happened, like running back to the large thirty-meter crater in hopes of finding lunar bedrock and being very disappointed when it wasn't there, or using the contingency sample staff to set the new lunar javelin throwing record. . . .

I believe that the message [of this flight] was that in the spirit of Apollo, a free and open spirit, you can attack a very difficult goal and achieve it if you can all agree on what the goal is. . . . I really had hoped, I think, that the impact would be more far-reaching than it has. Not that we haven't had a very great appreciation for the lunar landing around the world, and specifically in other countries; even the least developed of the countries, their appreciation has been equally great as here. But I had hoped that it might take our minds away from some of the more mundane and temporal problems that we as a society face, which are very similar to the problems that society of every age has faced, and look a little further into the future with an aim toward solving problems before they become problems. And, of course, the disadvantage of that is that by the time you react the problem has already occurred, and you're attacking it from the back side, so to speak, rather than meeting in head-on before it occurs. And, of course, this is a very inefficient way to solve problems, from the rear, catching up, so to speak. I think if we could all direct our attention a little further into the future, to try to foresee problems that are going to occur in the next years and decades, then perhaps we could be attacking these solutions from the front side when it's a great deal more easy to provide a viable solution and a meaningful one. . . .

I suspect that the space program as we know it is now inevitable. That is, it's a thing that now exists and will continue to exist for the rest of man's existence. We don't have the option any longer to say yes or no to it, we only have the option of saying when. Certainly there will be some questions as to how much is going to be done in the next year or the next ten years, or between now and the end of the millennium, but there is no question that throughout the history of man the moon will provide a very important function. It's difficult to say what it will be; but I'm certain people will go there, exist there, and conduct scientific experiments there, and, perhaps later, many more things.

# D i a n   F o s s e y

**1932–1985**

*"When you realize the value of all life, you dwell less on what is past and concentrate more on the preservation of the future."*

*Primatologist Dian Fossey was praised for her work among the great apes in Rwanda, where in 1967 she established Karisoke, a research camp to study the mountain gorillas of the region. Her efforts to communicate with the gorillas were finally rewarded when Peanuts, an adult male, touched her hand, marking the first friendly gorilla to human contact ever recorded. Observation and mimicry enabled Fossey to uncover new knowledge about the apes' behavior, whom she described as dignified, highly social "gentle giants." Fossey took an active stand against game wardens, zoo poachers, and government officials who threatened gorilla habitats, and when poachers killed a young male named Digit she waged a public campaign against gorilla poaching. She founded the Digit Fund, now the Dian Fossey Gorilla Fund, to provide a legacy of caring for the gorillas. Dr. Fossey was murdered in her cabin at Karisoke — presumably by poachers. The following is from her book,* Gorillas in the Mist.

There is a growing trend among conservationists, economists, sociologists, and journalists to approach the compounding problems of Third World countries more realistically than was advocated by the theorists of the past. This welcome trend is becoming increasingly widespread in conservation efforts in Africa, where until recently anachronistic conservation policies all but ignored the complexities of any country's bureaucracy, the basic needs of the human population, and the varying degrees of corruption among officials at a local level. Such disregard of reality has resulted in a form of short-lived innocuous diplomacy inhibiting resourcefulness and self-motivation among those most directly connected with the future of their country's wildlife. The self-eulogizing attempts of expatriots to impose the notion of wildlife as a treasured legacy overlook the reality that to most of a local impoverished and inert populace wildlife is considered an obstacle — tolerated only as long as it proves economically valuable on a practical basis in the form of tusks, meat, or skins.

On the other hand, promotion of tourism, if properly directed, might well prove profitable on a nationwide basis and thus compel the one-to-one reapers of wildlife proceeds to give way to the rule of the majority. This aim might be accomplished in Africa — a continent where tribalism, nepotism, and distinct class systems have evolved — only by consistent, uncompromising individuals able to consider the needs of the animals before their own.

Certainly, endangered species live on a day-to-day basis — be they the 242 mountain gorillas living in Africa, the 1,000 giant pandas remaining in China, or the 187 grizzly bears remaining in America. The survival chances of these species are little improved by tourism compared with more expedient actions that could be taken on their behalf. Active conservation includes frequent patrols in wildlife areas to destroy poacher equipment and weapons, firm and prompt law enforcement, census counts in regions of breeding and ranging concentration, and strong safeguards for the limited habitat the animals occupy. Such inglorious activities monetarily benefit no person, yet offer the diminishing number of animals in the forests an opportunity to survive into the future.

Methods of active conservation must necessarily be supplemented to longer-term projects. However, just as A comes before B, arduous daily conservation efforts must precede the Zs of theoretical conservation. In the case of the mountain gorilla, this means cutting traps and imprisoning convicted poachers; in the case of the giant pandas, this means thorough investigation of the availability of food resources; in the case of grizzly bears, this means strict enforcement of penalties against poachers and stringent surveillance of legal park boundaries.

I would like to express my heartfelt gratitude to the many intrepid Rwandese and Zairoise who have assisted me in realizing the expediency of today's aims toward the preservation of the mountain gorilla. For Digit, Uncle Bert, Macho, Lee, N'Gee, and so many other gorillas, I sorrow that I was too late to change the quixotic ways of many Europeans and Africans who, in hoping for a brighter dawn tomorrow, have yet to realize that avoidance of very basic conservation issues may ultimately push Beethoven, Icarus, Nunkie, their mates, and their progeny into the mountain mist of times past.

# David Ho

*"Nothing is more thrilling to me than the process of scientific discovery."*

*AIDS researcher Dr. David Ho was one of a small group of scientists who recognized that AIDS is an infectious disease, and set his research upon determining how HIV replicates in the body and invades immune cells. Two of his team's discoveries — that a particular gene mutation makes people resistent to invasion by HIV and that a triple combination of drugs can clear the bloodstream of detectable amounts of the virus — have made the development of effective vaccines and treatments a reality, and offered hope that maybe there could be a "cure" for AIDS in the next century. Although Ho's work is controversial in the scientific community, for his efforts he was hailed a wonderboy and* Time *magazine's Man of the Year in 1996. As we face a global epidemic of HIV infection, Dr. Ho is set upon inspiring government, academia, and the private sector to redouble its efforts to end what many are calling the plague of the new millennium.*

In our experiments attempting to eradicate HIV from an infected person, I have learned that success in research, as is the case in most endeavors, requires bold decision making and a willingness to take informed risks. You must take on the toughest challenge but view it as the greatest opportunity, for every noble work is at first seemingly impossible. Heed the wise words of Teddy Roosevelt before the turn of the century, "Far better it is to dare mighty things, to win glorious triumphs even though checkered by failure, than to rank with those poor spirits who neither enjoy nor suffer much because they live in the grey twilight that knows neither victory or defeat."

More and more, I have reflected on the role of science in our society. I am disturbed by the public's increasing indifference to what we do as scientists and engineers. As children, we all began with a real zest for science. We were intellectually curious, and provocative and insightful questions blurted out constantly. However, by early adulthood, this proclivity to science and the joy of discovery have somehow dissipated in most, only to be replaced by science phobia. Consequently, it is not surprising that our society has often stereotyped, unflatteringly, those scientists and engineers who carry out incomprehensible lines of work. Thomas Edison, Alexander Graham Bell, and the Wright Brothers would be today's nerds, even though the products of their ingenuity have made our world better. I am particularly saddened by the fact that many of my personal heroes in science are virtual unknowns to a typical citizen, while certain dubious characters are universally recognized and often glorified by our society. As scientists and engineers, we must change this by learning to present our work in both interesting and understandable ways. It is our responsibility to bring back the sense of wonder about nature that lies deep within every citizen.

I am equally troubled by society's lack of commitment to research in basic science. A former president said in a campaign speech, "Why should we subsidize intellectual curiosity?" This simple but naive question speaks volumes of the lack of appreciation of the richness that uninhibited fundamental research has brought us. Carl Sagan said it best when he wrote, "Maxwell wasn't thinking of radio, radar, and television when he first scratched out the fundamental equations of electromagnetism; Newton wasn't dreaming of space flight or communication satellites when he first understood the motion of the moon; Roentgen wasn't contemplating medical diagnosis when he investigated a penetrating radiation so mysterious he called it X rays; Curie wasn't thinking of cancer therapy when she painstakingly extracted minute amounts of radium from tons of pitchblende; Fleming wasn't planning on saving the lives of millions with antibiotics when he noticed a circle free of bacteria around a growth of mold; Watson and Crick weren't imagining the cure of genetic diseases when they puzzled over Z-ray diffractometry of DNA." These discoveries and a multitude of others that characterize our time were made by scientists given the opportunity to explore what in their opinion were basic questions in nature.

Despite the breakneck speed of scientific discoveries in the field, AIDS patients already faced a decade and a half of disappointment. But, because of science, there is new hope. In the past two years, with new knowledge and new therapies, it has become possible to control HIV so effectively that the virus is no longer detectable in the infected person. This dramatic attack on the virus is associated with a substantial clinical benefit to the patient. For the first time in this dreadful epidemic, the tide has begun to turn against the virus. Although a cure is still not in hand, the worst fear — the foreboding sense that the AIDS virus might be invincible — has finally been subdued. After years of cursing the darkness of AIDS, a candle of hope has been lit by science.

# Nellie Bly

*"Energy rightly applied and directed can accomplish anything."*

*Before the muckrakers, there was Nellie Bly. A pioneer of investigative journalism, Bly courted the American public as a reporter for the* New York World, *where she parlayed her blend of instinct, guts, and brutal honesty into shocking stories that scrutinized society and its ills. Famous for posing as an inmate to expose conditions of an insane asylum on New York City's Blackwell's Island and bettering the eighty-day record of the fictional Phineas Fogg by circling the globe in just seventy-two days, Bly won accolades as daredevil, social reformer, and "best reporter in America." The uninhibited Bly was also an industrialist — introducing the steel barrel to the distilling process in America and managing two "socially responsible" multimillion-dollar companies long before women CEOs and employee rights existed. Landing in Europe at the outbreak of World War I, Bly became the first woman to report from the eastern front. In 1919, the timeless words of her* New York Evening Journal *column inspired readers.*

If one would become great, two things are absolutely necessary. The first is to know yourself, and second is not to let the world know you.

If you do not know yourself, you are a slave. Your hands and feet are tied; your mouth is gagged; your eyes are blindfolded.

If the world knows you, you are a prey. Your heart and soul are exposed and unprotected; your abilities are undefended; your progress is defeated.

You could not expect to win a game if you did not know what cards you held.

Nor could you win it if your opponent knew your cards.

That parallel holds equally good in the game of life. You cannot win success if you do not know what cards you hold. In other words — your capabilities. Nor can you succeed if yourself is open and bare to the eyes and knowledge of the multitudes. To carry your heart upon your sleeve for daws to peck at is not nearly so fatal as to expose the you to the mercies of an intriguing and callous world.

Smiles, expressions, and words should be the shield or mask to protect you. By these means, one can avoid being the victim of the unscrupulous.

If you are an open book to the world, you are doomed. . . .

The secret of your control, of your power, of your abilities and inabilities, your omissions and commissions, your inclinations and dislikes, your weakness and your strength, are in the possession of others. The better the you is known the weaker you are, the less able to become powerful and successful.

Never forget: You cannot win a game if your opponent knows your hand — if he knows what you will play, if he knows what you think.

Just as certain is it, you cannot achieve success unless you know yourself. Study your abilities, analyze your character; realize your power.

This game of life is so beautiful. Taste the joy of finding and developing new powers within you and you will never crave other excitement or entertainment. Never stop! When you discover and expand one new little cell in your brain, find another. The possibilities are endless.

# John F. Kennedy

**1917–1963**

*"The New Frontier of which I speak is not a set of promises — it is a set of challenges. It sums up not what I intend to offer the American people, but what I intend to ask of them."*

*The youngest man elected president, the youngest to die in office, John F. Kennedy literally stole the hearts of a nation with his charm, vitality, and optimism. As president, Kennedy set out to deliver his campaign pledge to get America moving again. His economic programs launched the country on its longest sustained expansion since World War II; before his death, he laid plans for a massive assault on persisting pockets of poverty. He took vigorous action toward new civil rights legislation, and his vision extended to the quality of the national culture and the central role of the arts in society. His establishment of the Peace Corps moved the country toward his goal of "a world of law and free choice, banishing the world of war and coercion." The beginning of new hope and peace after two world wars, Kennedy's 1961 Inaugural Address offers the memorable injunction: "Ask not what your country can do for you — ask what you can do for your country."*

The world is very different now. For man holds in his mortal hands the power to abolish all forms of human poverty and all forms of human life. And yet the same revolutionary beliefs for which our forebears fought are still at issue around the globe — the belief that the rights of man come not from the generosity of the state, but from the hand of God.

We dare not forget today that we are the heirs of that first revolution. Let the word go forth from this time and place, to friend and foe alike, that the torch has been passed to a new generation of Americans — born in this century, tempered by war, disciplined by a hard and bitter peace, proud of our ancient heritage — and unwilling to witness or permit the slow undoing of those human rights to which this Nation has always been committed, and to which we are committed today at home and around the world. Let every nation know, whether it wishes us well or ill, that we shall pay any price, bear any burden, meet any hardship, support any friend, oppose any foe, in order to assure the survival and the success of liberty. . . .

Let us begin anew — remembering on both sides that civility is not a sign of weakness, and sincerity is always subject to proof. Let us never negotiate out of fear. But let us never fear to negotiate.

Let both sides explore what problems unite us instead of belaboring those problems which divide us.

Let both sides, for the first time, formulate serious and precise proposals for the inspection and control of arms — and bring the absolute power to destroy other nations under the absolute control of all nations.

Let both sides seek to invoke the wonders of science instead of its terrors. Together let us explore the stars, conquer the deserts, eradicate disease, tap the ocean depths, and encourage the arts and commerce.

Let both sides unite to heed in all corners of the earth the command of Isaiah — to "undo the heavy burdens . . . and to let the oppressed go free."

And if a beachhead of cooperation may push back the jungle of suspicion, let both sides join in creating a new endeavor, not a new balance of power, but a new world of law, where the strong are just and the weak secure and the peace preserved. All this will not be finished in the first 100 days. Nor will it be finished in the first 1,000 days, nor in the life of this Administration, nor even perhaps in our lifetime on this planet. But let us begin . . . .

Now the trumpet summons us again — not as a call to bear arms, though arms we need; not as a call to battle, though embattled we are — but a call to bear the burden of a long twilight struggle, year in and year out, "rejoicing in hope, patient in tribulation" — a struggle against the common enemies of man: tyranny, poverty, disease, and war itself.

Can we forge against these enemies a grand and global alliance, North and South, East and West, that can assure a more fruitful life for all mankind? Will you join in that historic effort?

In the long history of the world, only a few generations have been granted the role of defending freedom in its hour of maximum danger. I do not shrink from this responsibility — I welcome it. I do not believe that any of us would exchange places with any other people or any other generation. The energy, the faith, the devotion which we bring to this endeavor will light our country and all who serve it — and the glow from that fire can truly light the world.

And so, my fellow Americans: ask not what your country can do for you — ask what you can do for your country. My fellow citizens of the world: ask not what America will do for you, but what together we can do for the freedom of man.

# Georgia O'Keeffe

**1887–1986**

*"I think I'd rather let the painting speak for itself than help it with the word."*

American painter Georgia O'Keeffe created a distinctive artistic technique of isolating and magnifying familiar objects found in nature — namely botanicals, bleached bones, and icons from the New Mexico desert — and recasting them in innovative shapes and colors. Although she has been labeled a surrealist, a precisionist, a progressive, and a feminist who used female sexual imagery within her technique (a statement O'Keeffe herself denied), O'Keeffe's persona is not up for interpretation: she was individualistic and admired by many for her uncompromising lifestyle ("I simply paint what I see"). In 1946, after thirty years of drawing and painting, O'Keeffe was awarded the first artist retrospective ever held at the Museum of Modern Art in New York. Although her contribution to the modern art movement is defined as progressive, O'Keeffe's work provides a distinctively twentieth-century American perspective. She penned the following for one of her exhibition catalogues in the late 1930s.

A flower is relatively small. Everyone has many associations with a flower — the idea of flowers. You put out your hand to touch the flower — lean forward to smell it — maybe touch it with your lips without thinking — or give it to someone to please them. Still — in a way — nobody sees a flower — really — it is so small — we haven't time — and to see takes time like to have a friend takes time. If I could paint the flower exactly as I see it no one would see what I see because I would paint it small like the flower is small.

So I said to myself — I'll paint what I see — what the flower is to me but I'll paint it big and they will be surprised into taking time to look at it — I will make even busy New Yorkers take time to see what I see of flowers.

Well — I made you take time to look at what I saw and when you took time to really notice my flower you hung all your own associations with flowers on my flower and you write about my flower as if I think and see what you think and see of the flower — and I don't.

Then when I paint a red hill, because a red hill has no particular association for you like the flower has, you say it is too bad that I don't always paint flowers. A flower touches almost everyone's heart. A red hill doesn't touch everyone's heart as it touches mine and I suppose there is no reason why it should. The red hill is a piece of the bad lands where even the grass is gone. Bad lands roll away outside my door — hill after hill — red hills of apparently the same sort of earth that you mix with oil to make paint. All the earth colors of the painter's palette are out there in the many miles of bad lands. The light naples yellow through the ochres — orange and red and purple earth — even the soft earth greens. You have no associations with those hills — our waste land — I think our most beautiful country — You may not have seen it, so you want me always to paint flowers.

I fancy all this hasn't much to do with painting.

I have wanted to paint the desert and I haven't known how. I always think that I cannot stay with it long enough. So I brought home the bleached bones as my symbols of the desert. To me they are as beautiful as anything I know. To me they are strangely more living than the animals walking around — hair, eyes, and all with their tails switching. The bones seem to cut sharply to the center of something that is keenly alive on the desert even tho' [sic] it is vast and empty and untouchable — and knows no kindness with all its beauty.

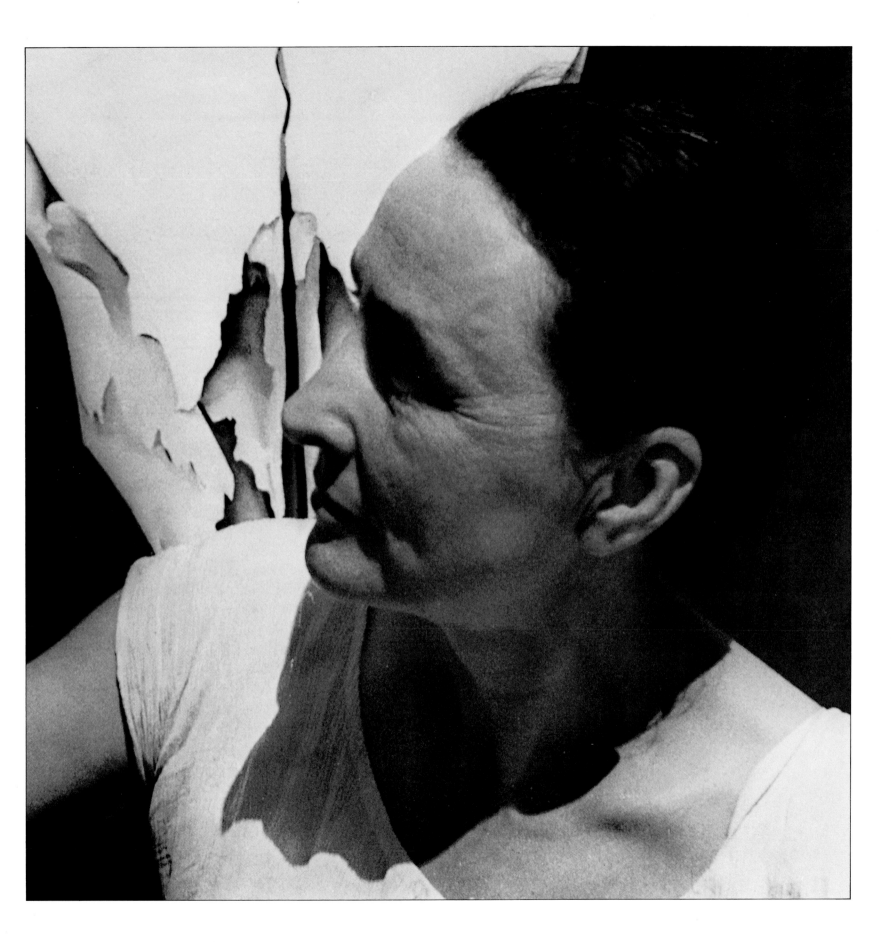

# Fred Rogers

b. 1928

*"You are the only person like you in this whole world. You are special. And people can like you just because you're you."*

*What makes a television personality a hero? In the half-century that television has been available to the American public, only a few stand out as truly heroic. Now celebrating his thirty-first season of* Mister Rogers' Neighborhood *on PBS, Fred Rogers is a pioneer who has become a legend. The soothing host of the popular television series for children makes us, young and old alike, feel safe, cared for, and valued as he helps us learn about feelings, values, friendship, and love. Fundamental to the premise of the program is each individual's self-worth. Mister Rogers genuinely cares about visitors to his "Neighborhood" — one might say he models the appreciation of individual worthiness that is fundamental to a ucessful multicultural society. Fads and fashion — in television and in society — change constantly, but the values to which Fred Rogers speaks are timeless and universal.*

Most of my childhood heroes wore capes, flew through the air, and picked up buildings with one arm. They were spectacular, and got a lot of attention. But as I grew, my heroes changed, and so now, to me, heroes are people who care enough about themselves and others that they recognize a moment of potential bitterness and turn it into a great opportunity.

A regret that I have carried for nearly fifty years has to do with not seeing one of my heroes, Dr. Martin Luther King Jr. I had bought my ticket to Selma, Alabama, for the civil rights march, to go along with some of my minister friends, but I couldn't get anyone to replace me at the television studio that day, where I was working on a local children's program. I missed an important part of American history and a chance to be in the presence of Dr. King, who was indeed a hero.

Typically, heroes are the stuff of tall tales and legends. But in our real world they are people of all ages, races, and cultures who are working to create hope where there seems to be despair — who are helping to make important changes in their own neighborhoods.

My cousin Betty was such a person. She and I were exactly the same age. We grew up together, like sister and brother. Twenty-five years ago, Betty got cancer and was plagued with it off and on . . . mostly on. But through all of her surgeries, all of her tests, all of her chemical therapies, she has consistently thought of her disease as a challenge. "If I hadn't been through it," she would say, "I wouldn't be able to help other people with it as much." And so she did. Her telephone was busy most of the time. Usually someone at the other end was just about to go through a new challenge, and Betty was there listening as well as cheering them on. When she was able, she visited cancer patients and cooked for their families — all this while raising her own family of sons and delighting in her grandchildren.

Once Betty was driving her car home from one of her many appointments, and just a block and a half from her home a young man drove through a stop sign and hit her broadside. The damage was several broken bones and a pierced lung . . . for Betty. She was in terrible pain, but from her hospital room she found out that the young man had been working a double shift to support his family. When he called her to apologize, she said she knew he didn't do it intentionally, and said to him, "I guess we were both at the wrong place at the wrong time."

Betty recovered from that accident, but several months later she started her last fight with the cancer, and soon she died. Everybody who knew her was convinced she had won. And we're all so much better for her having been in our midst.

From all that I can gather, that's the way it is with heroes — people like my cousin Betty and Dr. King — they transform the mundane into an opportunity to rejoice. I've also found such heroes in the children that I have met with over the years. Some are children who have defied unbeatable odds, but who are able to reach out and help others grow. Their sense of self-worth doesn't stop with "You are special," it includes, "and so is everyone else in this world." If we take the time to look and listen carefully, all around us we'll find people who are heroes, not only weathering the storms, but making beautiful days in their neighborhoods.

# S u s a n   B.   A n t h o n y

1820–1906

*"The true republic: men, their rights and nothing more; women, their rights and nothing less."*

*More than any woman over the course of history, Susan B. Anthony is responsible for the crusade for women's equality. Coined the Napoléon of the suffragist movement, Anthony forged the way for modern feminists of our time, speaking on behalf of the women of this nation when they had no voice. She relentlessly rallied to change the perception of the rights of women to a reticent nation, and addressed critical issues of fair political representation, domestic violence, birth control, divorce reform, and financial autonomy long before the concepts made their way into public consciousness. A dedicated campaigner and political reformer well into her eighties, she did not live long enough to see women win the right to vote. Once called a "manly woman" by her adversaries, she adopted the term to describe the woman of the future in an article she published at the turn of the century.*

We are all familiar with the ideal woman in vogue when I was young. Her portrait still exists in the family albums, and her prototype is faithfully reproduced in the pages of the harrowing novels on which she was wont to feed her intellect. Pale, delicate, sentimental, with the wasplike waist and a tendency to faint, she was the pet and plaything or the menial of man, typifying in her life and her attitude toward her husband, whom she ever regarded as a superior being. . . .

But evolution and woman herself have wrought a mighty change in the status of the sex, and now, at the dawning of the twentieth century, we have that product of modern civilization and progress known as the new woman, or the manly woman. She is not yet a perfect or fully developed creature, nor is her type so common that she has ceased to be the subject of the satirist, or the peg on which the humorist hangs his jokes. But she is here, and she has come to stay, and another generation will not only see her at her best, but vastly in the majority. Then, indeed, will civilization have reached a height of greatness as yet unknown to history. For a people is only as great, as free, as lofty, as advanced, as its women are free, noble, and progressive. It is the mothers who shape the destiny of the race. The manly woman of the new century will be an all-around being, with heart, body, mind, soul, and brain fully developed. She will be educated with her brother from the cradle till they have finished their college course, and she steps out from the halls of their alma mater, fully equipped with him to fight the battle of life and bring a practical, trained mind into a healthy body to bear upon the problems of the society and the commonwealth of which she is a part. . . .

The women of the twentieth century will possess, unchallenged, "the citizen's right to vote," and with it the power to make, shape, and control the situations surrounding her in the home, the church, and the state. The manly woman of this century will preside in her home with grace and dignity as the intellectual peer of any guest. If occasion demand, or the cook should leave without warning, she can also prepare the dinner, bringing both skill and science to her task: and she will have the backbone and the independence even to do the family washing in an emergency. . . .

The twentieth-century woman will know man for what he is — neither a monster of the iniquity to be shunned, nor a superior creature to be worshipped as an idol; not a lord and master to be cringingly obeyed, but a human being like herself, full of imperfections, but striving with all to make the world better for having lived it. She will be his equal partner in marriage, sharing fully in his joys and in his sorrows, in his prosperity as in his adversity, and whether, much or little, the half of what he has will be unquestioningly hers. . . .

The children of the manly woman and the womanly man of the twentieth century will be trained in the principles of good government. They will be taught that might is not right, either in the home or the state; that arbitration rather than human slaughter should settle all international difficulties, precisely as an individual should appeal to the justice of the courts instead of resorting to a brutal attack upon an enemy; and that the disfranchisement of one-half the people is a relic of barbarism not to be tolerated. . . .

I may not be here to witness the full fruition of this balancing of the sexes, but already we see the promise of its coming, and future generations will reap its blessings.

# Rosa Parks

b. 1913

*"I did not feel any fear at sitting in the seat I was sitting in. All I felt was tired. . . . I was just plain tired."*

*Rosa Louise Parks is national-ly recognized as the mother of the modern day civil rights movement in America. Her refusal to surrender her seat to a white male passenger on a Montgomery, Alabama, bus in 1955 birthed a wave of protest that washed over the United States. Her courageous act ulti-mately changed America and its view of African Americans, and redirected the course of history. After her arrest, organizers pro-moted a boycott of the city bus line under the leadership of Dr. Martin Luther King Jr. and the Montgomery Bus Boycott prompted a federal ruling that declared segregated bus service unconstitutional. A Congressional Gold Medal recipient, Parks continues to fight for human rights, working through her Rosa and Raymond Parks Institute for Self-Development to speak to the youth of America. A quiet exemplification of dignity and determination, Rosa Parks is a symbol to all Americans that one person can make a difference. She penned the following in her book* Quiet Strength.

On Thursday evening, December 1, I was riding the bus home from work. A white man got on, and the driver looked our way and said, "Let me have those seats." It did not seem proper, particularly for a woman to give her seat to a man. All the passengers just paid ten cents, just as he did. When more whites boarded the bus, the driver, J. P. Blake, ordered the blacks in the fifth row, the first row of the colored section (the row I was sitting in), to move to the rear. Bus drivers then had police powers, under both municipal and state laws, to enforce racial segregation. However, we were still sitting in the section designated for colored.

At first none of us moved.

"Y'all better make it light on yourselves and let me have those seats," Blake said.

Then three of the blacks in my row got up, but I stayed in my seat and slid closer to the window. I do not remember being frightened. But I sure did not believe I would "make it light" on myself by standing up. Our mistreatment was just not right, and I was tired of it. The more we gave in, the worse they treated us. I kept thinking about my mother and my grandparents, and how strong they were. I knew there was a possibility of being mistreated, but an opportunity was being given to me to do what I had asked of others.

I knew someone had to take the first step. So I made my mind not to move. Blake asked me if I was going to stand up.

"No. I am not," I answered.

Blake said that he would have to call the police. I said, "Go ahead." In less than five minutes, two police-men came and the driver pointed me out. He said that he wanted the seat and that I would not stand up.

"Why do you push us around?" I said to one of the policemen.

"I don't know," he answered, "but the law is the law and you're under arrest."

I did not get on the bus to get arrested; I got on the bus to go home. . . . I was just tired of giving in. Somehow, I felt that what I did was right by standing up to the that bus driver. I did not think about the consequences. I knew that I could have been lynched, manhandled, or beaten when the police came. I chose not to move. When I made that decision, I knew that I had the strength of my ancestors with me.

# William Faulkner

**1897–1962**

*"I decline to accept the end of man. . . . I believe that man will not merely endure: he will prevail."*

*When William Faulkner was awarded the 1949 Nobel Prize in literature, a few critics protested that his books were unworthy of such an honor. But the majority of the American public had long since come to appreciate Faulkner's raw portrayal of the human character, and embraced him as a quiet farmer-writer from Oxford, Mississippi. After* The Sound and the Fury *was published in 1929, Faulkner's stream of consciousness technique became accepted as a proper literary form, and Faulkner was recognized as one of the twentieth century's most gifted novelists. He took up screenwriting "to make ends meet," and soon claimed the film adaptations of* The Big Sleep *and Ernest Hemingway's novel* To Have and Have Not *as triumphs. Although Faulkner avoided speeches insisting "I'm just a farmer who likes to tell stories," as the first American novelist to accept the Nobel Prize since World War II, he recognized his unique obligation to speak his truth.*

I feel that this award was not made to me as a man, but to my work — a life's work in the agony and sweat of the human spirit, not for glory and least of all for profit, but to create out of the materials of the human spirit something which did not exist before. So this award is only mine in trust. It will not be difficult to find a dedication for the money part of it commensurate with the purpose and significance of its origin. But I would like to do the same with the acclaim too, by using this moment as a pinnacle from which I might be listened to by the young men and women already dedicated to the same anguish and travail, among whom is already that one who will some day stand where I am standing.

Our tragedy today is a general and universal physical fear so long sustained by now that we can even bear it. There are no longer problems of the spirit. There is only one question: When will I be blown up? Because of this, the young man or woman writing today has forgotten the problems of the human heart in conflict with itself which alone can make good writing because only that is worth writing about, worth the agony and the sweat.

He must learn them again. He must teach himself that the basest of all things is to be afraid: and, teaching himself that, forget it forever, leaving no room in his workshop for anything but the old verities and truths of the heart, the universal truths lacking which any story is ephemeral and doomed — love and honor and pity and pride and compassion and sacrifice. Until he does so, he labors under a curse. He writes not of love but of lust, of defeats in which nobody loses anything of value, of victories without hope and, worst of all, without pity or compassion. His griefs grieve on no universal bones, leaving no scars. He writes not of the heart but of the glands.

Until he learns these things, he will write as though he stood among and watched the end of man. I decline to accept the end of man. It is easy enough to say that man is immortal simply because he will endure: that when the last dingdong of doom has clanged and faded from the last worthless rock hanging tideless in the last red and dying evening, that even then there will still be one more sound: that of his puny inexhaustible voice, still talking. I refuse to accept this. I believe that man will not merely endure: he will prevail. He is immortal, not because he alone among creatures has an inexhaustible voice, but because he has a soul, a spirit capable of compassion and sacrifice and endurance. The poet's, the writer's, duty is to write about these things. It is his privilege to help man endure by lifting his heart, by reminding him of the courage and honor and hope and pride and compassion and pity and sacrifice which have been the glory of his past. The poet's voice need not merely be the record of man, it can be one of the props, the pillars to help him endure and prevail.

# Dolores Huerta

b. 1930

*"You ask me how I want to be remembered, what I want on my tombstone? 'Si se puede — it can be done!'"*

*Often described as the century's most powerful labor movement leader, Dolores Huerta is the cofounder and secretary-treasurer of the United Farm Workers of America (UFW). Borrowing inspiration from her mother, who owned a hotel that often housed farmworkers for free, Huerta has played many key roles in the UFW, including negotiating the first collective bargaining agreement for farmworkers, heading the UFW's national grape boycott with founder César Chavez, and directing the UFW's political and lobbying efforts. In championing farmworkers' rights, most recently to protect strawberry workers from the cancer-causing pesticide Captan, Huerta has often confronted "grower goons" and has been arrested more than twenty-two times for disobeying illegally imposed injunctions. Huerta, who led the struggle to achieve immigrant rights for farmworkers under the 1985 Rodino Amnesty Legalization Program, speaks to the necessity of using nonviolent social action to effect lasting change.*

When the farmworkers first started talking about nonviolence, I was organizing the first grape boycott in 1968, and Cesar was fasting. Everyone thought this was crazy. He continued to fast and decided to end it after twenty-five days. The farmworkers understood what he was doing — we had been on strike for three years — and he was trying to reach them. He was showing people that there is another way than violent revolution — by changing people's minds, by changing people's hearts, by changing people's behaviors. Then when he had his thirty-six day fast to get rid of pesticides, we were all really worried. But farmworkers' children were dying of cancer, and he felt he wasn't doing enough to raise the country's consciousness about the dangers of pesticides on our food.

President Abraham Lincoln held an unpopular position at the time by trying to abolish slavery. But he chose to follow his moral conscience, even amidst the societal pressures of his time. Although slavery was officially ended after the Civil War, we still have it with us in other forms. The farmworkers are a good example of that slavery that we see, where the people who do the most sacred work — they're out there every single day, in the heat, in the cold, preparing, planting, and harvesting the food at very low wages when they can't even feed themselves — are living really under a form of slavery. We see poverty in our society and that's really a form of violence.

We've got to redefine violence. What is violence? It's not just when somebody hits somebody, or wars, it's everything we see in society that makes people suffer — like racism, like homelessness, like poverty, like sexism. This is all violence against the helpless people of society. . . .

Farmworkers today are not protected. . . . [The government says] it's okay for farmworkers to be here, as long as we can treat them like slaves. They say we don't want people in our country who can be free, who can strike, who can vote for a union, who will be covered by the social legislation of our country, like unemployment insurance and social security. We want them only here as slaves. I think this is very frightening. . . .

In order to stop these policies that are coming down [from Congress], we really have got to make a strong, strong commitment to nonviolent action. And maybe there can be creative ways, like through marches. There's something about being together, about working together for a purpose. And that's what nonviolence is. Nonviolence is a very simple thing in many ways, but it's something that strengthens people and builds unity. It gives you a sense of empowerment you need to build those muscles — those psychic muscles that we need to get the job done.

We have to start thinking about what nonviolent actions we can do to stop these rotten policies that are racist and discriminatory, and anti–people of color. What can we do to make our public officials stop their actions? Some of us may have to do a fast somewhere; maybe we need to do more sit-ins. I can assure you right now that unless we start taking more active roles, things are just going to roll on and they're going to get very, very bad.

We try to follow the teachings of Gandhi. Anything we can do to follow those nonviolent actions are extremely important to the farmworkers' movement. . . . The thing about nonviolence is that it spreads. When you get people to participate in nonviolent action — whether it's a fast, a march, a boycott, or a picket line — people hear you, people see you, people are learning from that action.

# Thomas Edison

**1847–1931**

*"The best thinking has been done in solitude. The worst has been done in turmoil."*

*Inventor Thomas Alva Edison spent his life inventing many of the devices that shaped the modern American world. Dismissed from school at age seven because of his constant questioning of how things work, Edison flourished under nontraditional education and pure experimentation. After unsuccessfully trying to sell his first invention, an electric vote-recording machine, in 1868, Edison vowed to "work only on inventing things people would buy." It was his carbon transmitter that made fellow entrepreneur Alexander Graham Bell's telephone practical. With "one percent inspiration and 99 percent perspiration," the Wizard of Menlo Park invented the first phonograph and the prototype of the incandescent electric light bulb. These and other inventions — a storage battery, a dictaphone, and a mimeograph — led to his international acclaim, and by the late 1880s he was contributing to the development of silent motion pictures and later to talkies. The holder of over one thousand patents, he lived out his final years in a round of awards and honors.*

In my own case, [deafness] has been responsible, I think, for the perfection of the phonograph; and it had something to do with the development of the telephone into usable form. When Bell first worked out his telephone idea I tried it and the sound which came through the instrument was so weak I couldn't hear it. I started to develop it and kept on until the sounds were audible to me. I sold my improvement, the carbon transmitter, to the Western Union and they sold it to Bell. It made the telephone successful. If I had not been deaf it is possible and even probable that this improvement would not have been made. The telephone as we now know it might have been delayed if a deaf electrician had not undertaken the job of making it a practical thing.

The phonograph never would have had been what it now is and for a long time has been if I had not been deaf. Being deaf, my knowledge of sounds had been developed till it was extensive and I knew that I was not and no one else was getting overtones. Others working in the same field did not realize this imperfection, because they were not deaf. Deafness, pure and simple, was responsible for the experimentation which perfected the machine. It took me twenty years to make a perfect record of piano music because it is full of overtones. I now can do it — just because I'm deaf. . . .

Which do I consider my most famous invention? Well, my reply to that would be that I like the phonograph best. Doubtless this is because I love music. And then it has brought so much joy into millions of homes all over this country, and, indeed, all over the world. Music is so helpful to the human mind that it is naturally a source of satisfaction to me that I have helped in some way to make the very finest music available to millions who could not afford to pay the price and take the time necessary to hear the greatest artists sing and play.

Many inventions are not suitable for the people at large because of their carelessness. Before a thing can be marketed to the masses, it must be made practically foolproof. Its operation must be made extremely simple. That is one reason, I think, why the phonograph has been so universally adopted. Even a child can operate it.

Another reason, is that people are far more willing to pay for being amused than for anything else. . . .

I continually experiment with the phonograph, constantly improving it. There are those who fear that radio will kill it as a salable devise, but I know better. People will continue to want to hear what they want to hear when they want to hear it. They will continue to prefer what they hear without rather than with static and other interruptions and distractions. They will continue to desire to have carefully selected voices and well-chosen instrumentalists ready for their entertainment, rather than to trust to luck the program-arranger at a broadcasting station.

# Ella Fitzgerald

*"It isn't where you came from; it's where you're going that counts."*

*First Lady of Song Ella Fitzgerald is loved for the trademarks that defined her fifty-plus years of song-making magic: her mastery of scat singing, her inventive improvisations, her rare sweetness of voice. The tenacious young singer who rose up from the streets of Harlem to become this century's most recognized female jazz-pop vocalist claimed no special secrets other than "I just sing what I feel." She evolved from her early days touring with the Chick Webb Orchestra to a world-wide solo performer whose range included pop ballads, novelty tunes, 1940s bebop exploration, and classic 1950s "song book" recordings of tunes by Cole Porter, George and Ira Gershwin, and Duke Ellington. Refusing to be associated with any one type of music, she recorded some 250 albums that blended her styles together into an unprecedented persona of legend, heroine, and lover of song. The following lyrics are from her 1930 hit, "A-tisket A-tasket."*

A-tisket, a-tasket,
A green and yellow basket.
I bought a basket for my mommie,
On the way I dropped it.
I dropped it, I dropped it,
Yes, on the way I dropped it.
A little girl picked it up
And took it to the market.
She was truckin' on down the avenue,
Without a single thing to do.
She was peck, peck, peckin' all around,
When she spied it on the ground.

A-tisket, a-tasket,
She took my yellow basket,
And if she doesn't bring it back,
I think that I shall die.
(Was it red?) No, no, no, no.
(Was it brown?) No, no, no, no.
(Was it blue?) No, no, no, no.
Just a little yellow basket.

# Magic Johnson

b. 1959

*"Don't stop living. Enjoy life."*

*In 1991 Earvin "Magic" Johnson announced to a stunned and breathless nation that he was HIV-positive and retiring from the Lakers. Since then, he has returned to the NBA twice and retired twice — surprising teammates and fans alike. The three-time NBA Most Valuable Player, who led the Lakers to five NBA championships in the 1980s, is living generously and fruitfully. As part-owner in the Lakers, he performs his new roles as successful businessman, AIDS advocate, and public speaker. Johnson has directed his efforts toward his growing business empire, Magic Johnson Enterprises, through which he is staking his claim in challenged communities and revitalizing the local economies, including opening a chain of movie theaters in economically disadvantaged areas such as his own Crenshaw district of Los Angeles. As part of his job as an educator, he often visits inner-city high schools with a message to black youth.*

Basketball was my ticket to success. But if I hadn't been good enough, I would have been successful in something else. I would have gone to college, and worked hard, and made something of myself. You can do that, too.

Basketball is not the best way to get ahead. It's probably the most difficult path you could take. There are 27 teams in the NBA, and each team has 12 players. That makes 324 who are in the league at any one time. In a country as big as ours, that's not a big number. There are about 1,800 college seniors who play ball, and only a few of them are good enough to be drafted. So even if you're good enough and fortunate enough to play in college, what makes you think you're going to play in the NBA? You have to understand that your chances of playing basketball for a living are minuscule.

The black community already has enough basketball players. And enough baseball players, and football players. But there are a lot of other people we could really use. We need more teachers. We need more lawyers. We need more doctors. We need more accountants. We need more nurses. We need more pilots. We need more scientists. And more carpenters. And more professors. And more police officers. And more bankers. And more computer programmers. And more mechanics. And more social workers. And more car dealers. And more politicians.

And every single one of these professions — including doctor and lawyer — is easier to get into than the NBA.

There was a time when blacks couldn't do some of these things, and when sports and entertainment were the best ways to get ahead. That's not true anymore. Today, you have an opportunity to get ahead in many different areas. . . .

If you can possibly go to college, go! I know it's hard. I know that some kids you know will discourage you. If you're ambitious, if you study hard, if your goals are high, some people may tell you you're "acting white." Stay away from those people! They are not your friends. If the people around you aren't going anywhere, if their dreams are no bigger than hanging out on the corner, of if they're dragging you down, get rid of them. Negative people can sap your energy so fast, and they can take your dreams from you, too. . . .

I don't mean to tell you it's easy. It's not easy. Growing up today is hard. I know that. It's much harder than when I was your age. When I was a kid, there weren't many gangs. Or many guns. There was nothing like crack. Maybe you smoked a little pot, but that was it. Today there's cocaine, heroin, AIDS, all kinds of things that we didn't ever worry about. You might be an excellent student, but you're still living in fear because a stray bullet could hit you.

All of that is real. So is racism. Racism exists, but too often we use it as an excuse. I'm not saying it isn't there, because it definitely is. But if you get your education, you can look beyond that. I don't care what somebody calls you. You can still walk tall because of who you are.

If we keep using that same old excuse, that every time we fail it's because of racism, we'll never get ahead. We'll stay on the bottom. We've got to quit making excuses. Quit feeling sorry for ourselves. We have to go to college. Think about business. Work hard. Support one another, like other groups do.

The government will not save you.

The black leadership will not save you.

You're the only one who can make the difference.

Whatever your dream is, go for it.

# M a r g a r e t   M e a d

**1901–1978**

*"A knowledge of one other culture should sharpen our ability to scrutinize more steadily, to appreciate more lovingly, our own."*

*In 1928, anthropologist Margaret Mead published the landmark controversial study* Coming of Age in Somoa, *a soon-to-be best-seller that concluded that culture was the primary determinant of adolescent behavior. Named the "Mother of the World" by* Time *magazine in 1969, Mead is best known for establishing social anthropology as a science in the twentieth century — and for making it accessible to the nonacademic. She invited millions of people to look at the lives of other cultures, knowing that to do so would broaden their perspective of the world and their place in it. Her frank observations of the generation gap, family roles, sex, nuclear arms proliferation, the role of women in the church, the rights of the terminally ill, and male-female relationships transformed her into a guru of contemporary issues. A firm believer in the need for a single world language as a common base of communication to unify all people, Mead spoke to the danger of egocentricism as a nation and as individuals.*

In those rare moments of national triumph or tragedy in which everyone feels united, all Americans become "we." Certainly we as a nation sorrowed when President Kennedy was shot down and we as a people triumphed on the day of the first moon walk.

At other times "we" may represent only one's own family or, very narrowly, only one's own social, religious, ethnic, or racial group. The interesting thing is that most people do continually shift their stance and identify themselves with a great variety of groups, each of which becomes "we" in one context or another. The "we" classification changes as our perspective on the world changes, now expanding to include all human beings and now contracting to "thee and me."

In contrast to those with whom we identify, there are those whom we call "they" — a vague and anonymous "they" whose interests by definition are opposed to whatever "we" ourselves stand for. "They" litter the streets; "they" are against civil rights; "they" spread destructive rumors in a crisis and hoard food in times of scarcity; "they" condone bribery and corruption in high places. "They," clearly, are outsiders who all too often are to blame when "we" fail.

Children who are continually told not to behave like the So-and-so children down the block will always have a hard time finding a wider "we" group. Other people, different from themselves in appearance, speech, education, wealth, or manners, have come to represent an evil and rejected part of themselves, a part against which their parents continually warned them when they appeared, inappropriately, with dirty hands and uncombed hair, used "bad" grammar or "bad" language, slouched instead of standing up straight or expressed radical or other ideas considered unacceptable.

A first requirement in bringing up children who will find it easy to share a common humanity with others who are different in their appearance, education, and aspirations is never to exclude as different from our own group the child whose behavior we disapprove of. By pointing out that the child down the street who never is clean and screams dirty words is an outsider — is poor or has drug-addicted parents or belongs to a different ethnic, racial, or religious group — we convey to our children the idea that "they," who are unlike ourselves, are everything "we" reject in ourselves.

In wartime, when we feel that our country's safety may be at stake, our fellow citizens become "we" because we value them as fellow citizens. But at the same time millions of people who before were only vaguely "not us" become dangerously "they" — enemies whom it is moral and patriotic to kill.

The growth of civilization has been a history of including more people, and more diverse people, in the category of "we." But the scope of the "theys" whom we cannot trust and who may want to destroy us has increased simultaneously. Our best hope is that we can come to care positively about the diversity of human beings and ally ourselves with many different groups, all of whom we think of as "we." But until we do better at accepting our own faults and failures along with our successes, I do not know whether we shall be able to recognize that "they" are also "we."

# Louis Armstrong

**1900–1971**

*"All I want to do is live — good or bad, just live. . . . Like I always say, it's better to be 'once was' than 'never was.'"*

*Rare is the musician whose career has spanned a lifetime of eras. From turn-of-the-century New Orleans and the Roaring 1920s to the turbulent 1960s, innovative trumpeter and singer Louis Armstrong took the world by storm soon after he learned to make music. Raising himself up from a childhood of poverty, Armstrong made his name among the jazz greats of New York and Chicago and by the end of the 1920s "Satchmo" was billed as "the World's Greatest Trumpeter." Revered for shaping the development of jazz over several decades, and known worldwide for his rendition of "Hello Dolly," Armstrong spoke out against President Eisenhower when he witnessed the forced desegregation of Little Rock, Arkansas's Central High School; despite the controversy that surrounded him during the civil rights era, Armstrong spent the 1960s traveling abroad as the goodwill ambassador of jazz for America.*

*A prolific writer, Armstrong mused often about life, love, and the endurance of music.*

These cool cats that say my music's old fashioned. They say they study music. Funny they got to and I didn't have to go into no fundamentals. More power to them. If I'm out of style now, I was a flying cat when I was in — so to hell with it now. If a son-of-a-bitch came to the conclusion, "We don't ever want to see Louis Armstrong again" — Thank you! 'cause I can get in a corner, look at TV for days, and take my shower, sleep, and let the maid come in, don't even look out the window for six months. I'll still be Satchmo. Ain't never going to move. That's the way I can enjoy life. I don't sign for nothing. Sixty years is a long time and there ain't going to be no more cats in the game that long.

Jazz is all the same — isn't anything new. At one time they was calling it levee camp music, then in my day it was ragtime. When I got up North I commenced to hear about jazz, Chicago style, Dixieland, swing. All refinements of what we played in New Orleans. But every time they change the name, they got a bigger check. And all these different kinds of fantastic music you hear today — course it's all guitars now — used to hear that way back in the old sanctified churches where the sisters used to shout till their petticoats fell down. There ain't nothing new. Old soup used over. . . .

So now a lot of stars picking up the old records, and phrasing from them, and making hits. Ain't a trumpet player alive that don't play a little something I used to play. Makes them feel like they're getting hot or something. Real Negroid. That's all right. Makes me feel good.

I don't think you should analyze music. Like the old timer told me, he say, "Don't worry about that black cow giving white milk. Just drink the milk."

You know, I haven't heard no band that plays more perfect music than Guy Lombardo yet. That's the way I feel, and I don't let my mouth say nothing my head can't stand. I dug that band when they first came from Canada and I used to go out many nights where they were on Cottage Grove in Chicago. People would say, surprised like, "You sitting in with them?" I'd try to tell them, music is music. That band plays the tune, they put that melody there, and it's beautiful. You can't find another band that can play a straight lead and make it sound that good. . . .

I've had some great ovations in my time. When people do that, they must feel something within themselves. I mean you don't just go around waking people up to the effect of saying, "You know, this music is art." But it's got to be art because the world has recognized our music from New Orleans, else it would have been dead today. But I always let the other fellow talk about art. 'Cause when we was doing it, we was just glad to be working up on that stage. So for me to be still on earth to hear that word, sounds pretty good. I'm just grateful for every little iota.

Some cats wants pats on the back, and they wants you to kneel down 'cause they did this and did that and they are so and so. But I still feel I'm just an ordinary human being trying to enjoy the work I live. It's something to know you still can make that call when the man say, "All on." That's enough wonderment for me. A lot of 'em is gone, dropped out. Ain't but a few left, a few of us.

# Gloria Steinem

b. 1934

*"I define feminism as 'the belief that women are full human beings.'"*

*Credited with nearly thirty years of contribution to women's equality, feminist leader Gloria Steinem is best known for her writing, her efforts as an organizer and lecturer, and the launching of the landmark magazine* Ms. *Perhaps more heroically she has spearheaded a controversial political movement for reproductive freedom and the Equal Rights Amendment, helped to overhaul the language Americans use to describe women, and recast the feminist movement for the 1990s and beyond. A prolific organizer, Steinem co-established the Ms. Foundation for Women, the Coalition of Labor Union Women, and the National Women's Political Caucus. Her thoughts and writings form a lasting legacy of heroic ideas that challenge women and girls to claim gender equality as a part of this nation's contemporary history. In 1997, she wrote to the next generation of women about planting seeds for another twenty-five years of progress.*

I don't regret one moment of those early firecracker days when explosions of consciousness lit up the sky. Somewhere, women go through them again every day when they discover how much of the female experience is political, not inevitable. Even we golden oldies reexperience this excitement when new perceptions and issues arise. But bursts of light tend to flatten out the subtlety of differences between and among women, and a movement fueled only by adrenaline burns out its members — as many of us can testify.

On the other hand, younger women and newer activists checked into a world that already has a degree of feminist consciousness. They have higher expectations and an acute awareness of the backlash to the growing power of the women's movement. They generate a steadier light that exposes the tangled patterns of race, class, sexuality, and physical ability in women's lives. Where my generation externalized almost everything and used this energy to confront injustice, younger and later activists admit how much of that injustice has been internalized, and use this energy to dig deeper into individual psyches and family patterns. Where we risked repeating the same behavior because we hadn't dug out its personal and family roots, they risk recreating a social pattern because they neglected its politics.

Thanks to feminist parents as well as to women's studies and a popular culture that occasionally pays tribute to a feminist worldview, the new generation has a better idea of the complexity involved in making lasting change. But now, that's countered by a soundbite culture, and a resistance to equality that is ever ready with terms like "postfeminism," which makes no more sense than "postdemocracy."

Without the excitement and mutual support of early, small-group feminism, I fear this and future generations won't have the personal rewards and fireworks that hooked us for a lifetime. On the other hand, without large organizations to turn out the vote and raise money to keep generations of struggle going, suffragists and abolitionists couldn't have won — and we can't either.

That's why, old or young, experienced or brand-new, we have to achieve balance in the next quarter-century: between present and future, external and internal, spontaneity and long-term planning. We have to get beyond either/or to and; beyond ranking to linking; beyond such labels as "equality feminists" versus "difference feminists," and into a full circle of tactics that surround the goal instead of approaching it from one direction. We need both excitement and steadiness, small feminist support groups and national organizations, bursts of new consciousness that are rewards in themselves and the satisfaction of repeating what has been planned and perfected.

To accomplish this, we're going to need crazy women marching in the street who make women working inside seem reasonable, and inside negotiators who turn street demands into practical alternatives; radical feminists who confront the roots of injustice, and liberal feminists who build bridges for reforms that are radical in the long term; feminists who focus on the shared origins of sexism, racism, and homophobia, and feminists who work in intimate depth within their own communities; feminist economists who take on the System of National Accounts plus the structural readjustment of poorer nations' debt, and women who expose their own childhood sexual abuse in order to end abusive cycles that have made generations of women believe, "I'm good for nothing else."

Your part in this next quarter-century depends on the groups, issues, and styles that make you feel supported, angry, inspired, or energized . . . into becoming a long-distance runner. . . . I hope to be with you — dreaming, fighting, planning, laughing, and transforming all the way. But as Elizabeth Cady Stanton understood at seventy-two, with no chance of living to see victory: if any of us make it, we all will.

# William and Kathleen Magee

b. 1944  b. 1945

*"In life, there are no ordinary moments. Most of us never really recognize the most significant moments of our lives when they're happening."*

*In 1982, plastic surgeon Dr. Bill Magee and his wife Kathy, a nurse and clinical social worker, founded Operation Smile, a not-for-profit organization that dispatches volunteer medical teams to developing countries to perform free reconstructive facial surgery on disfigured children. The Magees have taken their talents to the inner cities of Panama, the rural villages of the Philippines, and the war-torn cities of Vietnam with a simple goal in mind: "To give children a chance, before it's too late for them to make something of their lives." What started out as a single journey to the Philippines seventeen years ago has turned into a global humanitarian effort. To date, the Magees and their Operation Smile teams have launched more than 240 medical trips to 20 countries — all in all, performing miracles on over 50,000 kids. They feel their mission statement is a modest one: to change the face of the world, one smile at a time.*

Ours has been a journey of discovery. As we've experienced and grown and changed, we've discovered that love, by definition, is self-sacrifice. Love is a decision to make someone else's problem your problem. It's putting someone else's needs above your own. We see this every day in our travels, in the tender way doctors cradle babies and in the graceful way families embrace our presence. As visitor and host, we come together for a single purpose — a single purpose, driven by love.

On every Operation Smile mission, we are accompanied by people who are there to help carry the load, comfort the suffering, plead for the hopeless, uplift the fallen, and befriend the friendless. From them, we have learned about love. From more than 50,000 children and families who have so humbly placed their lives, and their hopes, in our hands, we have learned about love. We witnessed love in the father who traveled twenty-four hours by foot across mountains, rivers, and jungles with his daughter on his back, hoping to meet a foreign doctor who could save her life. We felt love from the young man with a terrible deformity who pushed away his own chance for care so a child — a total stranger — could start life anew at a much younger age. And we knew it was love that would guide us as we promised a mother that we would return to help the children who would still be waiting for us in five or ten years' time.

It's by allowing love to drive us, emotion rather than reason, that we have made a difference in our lives as well as in the lives of others. Because no amount of knowledge will ever nurture or sustain your spirit. It will never provide you ultimate happiness or peace. It's only when knowledge is infused with intense feeling and constant energy that knowledge comes alive. Likewise, it's not logic that solves any problem. Logically, we all know what's right and wrong. It's not until we feel a passion in our hearts that we're called into action.

And we have been called into action. We believe the world can be changed if we focus on the things we can do, rather than the things we can't do. The success of our life mission supports that. Whether it's time, talent, or treasure, we know we really only keep that which we give away. Only through the sacrifice of those who offer of themselves so generously have we been able to bridge countries, cultures, communities, and families — and to love. And, in turn, be loved back.

For eighteen years we have traveled the world. Yet it has often only been in hindsight that we've see the significant results of our ordinary deeds: the short surgery that has freed a child from deformity and ultimately frees a village from shame, the simple sacrifice of a few days and a few dollars that result in a lifetime of hope. We have seen children's faces change through surgery, and we have seen their parents' faces change through gratitude. We have watched sons be able to kiss their mothers for the very first time and have seen fathers when they recognize the new beauty in their daughters' faces.

These are the ordinary moments when love is shared. And the extraordinary results that come from that sharing. When we come together, we find the bond that embraces us all.

# Marian Wright Edelman

b. 1939

*"Service is the rent we pay for living."*

*Marian Wright Edelman, founder and president of the Children's Defense Fund, has been an advocate for disadvantaged Americans her entire career. Under her leadership the CDF has become a strong national voice for children, seeking for every child a healthy start, a head start, a fair start, a safe start, and a moral start in life. As the first black woman admitted to the Mississippi Bar, the Yale School graduate directed the NAACP Legal Defense and Educational Fund office in Jackson, Mississippi. She founded the Washington Research Project, a public interest law firm and the parent body of the CDF. In 1996, Edelman founded Stand for Children, which brings together children's rights activists from across the country.*

*On the steps of the Lincoln Memorial on the first Stand for Children Day in 1996, Edelman challenged Americans "to put children first, to build a just America that leaves no child behind, and to ensure all our children a healthy and safe passage into adulthood."*

Together we can give our children back their childhoods, safety, and hope to improve millions of young lives right now. While we don't know yet how the brain works or have a cure for AIDS, we do know how to prevent and treat many childhood diseases and provide quality health care, child care, parent education, and recreation. We just need to do more of what we know works for all our children. . . .

We stand today from across the nation because we know . . . we are the answer — individuals, families, community, religious leaders, and citizens who hold ourselves personally accountable and who hold our leaders publicly accountable with our voices and votes. As active citizens, we can make our leaders help rather than hinder our children and make it easier rather than harder for families to raise healthy, safe, educated, and moral children. We can and must end the simplistic either/or political and media labels that get in the way of meeting complex and varying child and family needs.

Children require a seamless web of family, community, employer, and government support. All children need strong family and social values; private charity and social justice; good home training, good school training, good job training, and good moral training; and parents and leaders who struggle to practice what they preach. So many of our children are morally confused because so many adults talk right and do wrong in our private, professional, and public lives.

Just as President Lincoln's memorial is undergoing repair and renovation from the ravages of wear, weather, and time, our nation's spiritual, economic, and social values and public discourse need repair from the ravages of resurging racism, intolerance, violence, and extremism. We have seen our national house of law exploded in Oklahoma City and God's houses of worship torched in Alabama and Tennessee. We hear voices of division dishonoring the sacrifices of Gettysburg, Birmingham, and Mississippi and of Lincoln and King who lived and died for "one nation under God, indivisible, with liberty and justice for all." We will stand up to those who try to divide America into two houses: one for "them" and one for "us." We will stand strong for one national house big enough and fair enough for the privileged and powerful, the struggling middle class, and the poor and powerless. We stand for one strong national safety net for our old, disabled, and sick during recession, disaster, and joblessness wherever they live. . . .

President Lincoln warned that "a house divided against itself cannot stand." That's why we remember his words and are acting to renovate our divided and battered national house to make sure it has room and justice enough for all. When Jesus Christ invited little children to come unto him, He did not invite only rich, middle class, male, white children without mental or physical challenges, from two-parent families. . . . He invited all children to come as do all the great faiths . . . to renew America's and God's sacred covenant with every child. . . .

It is always the right time to do right for our children being born and formed in mind, body, and spirit every minute as life goes on or stops. In the six hours since 9:00 A.M. when we began Stand for Children Day, one American child has died from child abuse and neglect, four have died from gunshots, and seven have died from poverty. Twenty-three infants have died before their first birthday, and four hundred have decided to drop out of school. America can do better. The can-do America which wrestled independence from the British, sent the first human to the moon, stopped Hitler's and Mussolini's war on human decency can stop child suffering and death and save our children, families, and communities. A nation that does not stand up for its children does not stand for anything and will not stand strong in the twenty-first century.

# Henry Ford

1863–1947

*"I will build a motor car for the great multitude . . . no man making a good salary will be unable to own one and enjoy with his family hours of pleasure in God's great open spaces."*

*Pioneer, inventor, and philosopher, Henry Ford symbolizes the individualism and productive genius cornerstone to the development of this country. After he witnessed a traveling steam engine that moved along the road by its own power, Ford's boyhood dream of a "horseless carriage" manifested in the creation of the gas-engine-powered Quadricycle in 1896. With words of encouragement from fellow inventor Thomas Edison ("Young man, you have it, a self-contained unit carrying its own fuel, keep at it!"), Ford left his post at the Detroit Edison Illuminating Company to pursue his hobby: building automobiles. On June 16, 1903, with ten investors and his patents, knowledge, and engine, Henry Ford incorporated the Ford Motor Company. Famous today for the classic Model T and the development of the assembly line, Ford sold more than one-half of the cars in the industry between 1910 and 1930. The rest, as they say, is history.*

There is no denying the fact that life seems to be becoming more complicated. But is it, really? Isn't it rather that we are asked to make decisions more rapidly than before? With our new forms of transportation and communication the whole outlook of man is changed. It is greatly enlarged. He travels more, sees more, comes in contact with more people, does more things. But there is a question in my mind whether, with all this speeding up of our everyday activities, there is any more real thinking. Thinking is the hardest work there is, which is the probable reason why so few engage in it. If it were possible first to teach people how to go to work to think, and then to think, there would be hope for all sorts of things.

It is easy to have ideas. But whose are they and what are they worth? Merely having something on your mind is not thinking. Merely wondering is not thinking. Merely worrying is not thinking. Merely listening with all intentness to catch and remember something that someone is offering out of the essence of wisdom is not thinking. We all have intelligence, for intelligence is the ability to receive; but we have little thinking.

Thinking is creative or it is analytical. Intelligence comprehends the outlines of a thing. Thinking breaks it into its elements, analyzes it, and puts it together again. One feels, however, that — regardless of the fact that up to the present time everything has been about all that it could be under the circumstances — there is a sense in which from this moment forward a new era may emerge, if the necessary human components of the new era decide so. Perhaps the most one can hope for now is to drive home a conviction that as a people we have not done much thinking. If we think we have been thinking and then find out that we have not, the jolt of discovery may be of service to us.

The secrets of life are open to the thinker. Thinking is the work of digging to the foundation and has the aid of higher lights. Thinking calls for facts, and facts are found by digging. He who has gathered of this wealth is well-equipped for life.

Of course, in the long run we never really create anything new. We merely discover something which has already existed. We know when we have reached Truth. We are on the right road toward Truth when the things that we are doing make men a little freer than they were. We may also know when we are on the right road by examining what our motives are. Of course, mistakes may be committed with right motives, but the general direction is right when the motive is right. These are the things of which we may be perfectly sure. These principles surround the very basis of Life. . . .

Our experiences are coming faster than ever before, both in our industrial world and in our domestic life. Many people see in these changes a world constantly growing worse. I do not believe this; I think we are headed in the right direction and that we should learn to interpret our new life rather than protest against it. We are entering a new era. Old landmarks have disappeared. Our new thinking and new doing are bringing us to a new world, a new heaven, and a new earth, for which prophets have been looking from time immemorial. Much of it is here already. But I wonder if we see it.

# Clara Barton

**1821–1912**

*"Living is doing."*

*An adventurous and strong-willed nurse aided the International Red Cross in Europe during the Franco-Prussian War. There she found a humanitarian model for dealing with the atrocities of war, and returned to the United States campaigning for the establishment of an American Red Cross. Although she would rather have been a soldier in the Civil War, Clara Barton was the Angel of the Battlefield — doling out bandages made from bedsheets, wrapping wounds, and raising spirits as she combated calamity, plague, famine, and fire. She defined nursing as a profession, establishing it as a trained, paid occupation rather than a menial service relegated to women during times of war. The founder of the most significant philanthropic movement of the age and the first to organize relief for natural disasters, Barton expended her energies in the field through age seventy-nine, when she served during Texas's Galveston flood. In her appeal to Congress for the establishment of the Red Cross, Barton distributed these words in a self-published pamphlet.*

A confederation of relief societies in different countries, acting under the Geneva convention, carries on its work under the sign of the Red Cross. The aim of these societies is to ameliorate the condition of wounded soldiers in the armies in campaigns on land or sea. . . .

These national relief societies . . . afford ready succor and assistance to sufferers in time of national or widespread calamities, such as plagues, cholera, yellow fever, and the like, devastating fires or floods, railway disasters, mining catastrophes, etc. The readiness of organizations like those of the Red Cross to extend help at the instant of need renders the aid of quadruple value and efficiency compared with that gathered hastily and irresponsibly, in the bewilderment and shock which always accompanies such calamities. The trained nurses and attendants subject to the relief societies in such cases would accompany the supplies sent and remain in action as long as needed. Organized in every state, the relief societies of the Red Cross would be ready with money, nurses, and supplies to go on call to the instant relief of all who were overwhelmed by any of those sudden calamities which occasionally visit us. In the case of yellow fever, there being an organization in every state, the nurses and attendants would be first chosen from the nearest societies, and, being acclimated, would incur far less risk to life than if sent from distant localities.

It is true that the government is always ready in these times of public need to furnish transportation, and often does much more. In the Mississippi flood, a few years ago, it ordered rations distributed under the direction of army officers; in the case of the explosion at the navy yard, it voted a relief fund, and in our recent affliction at the South, a like course was pursued. But in such cases one of the greatest difficulties is that there is no organized method of administering the relief which the government or liberal citizens are willing to bestow, nor trained and acclimated nurses ready to give intelligent care to the sick; or, if there be organization, it is hastily formed in the time of need, and is therefore comparatively inefficient and wasteful.

It would seem to be full time that, in consideration of the growth and rapidly accumulating necessities of our country, we should learn to economize our charities, and ensure from them the greatest practical benevolence. Although we in the United States many fondly hope to be seldom visited by the calamities of war, yet the misfortunes of other nations with which we are on terms of amity appeal to our sympathies; our southern coasts are periodically visited by the scourge of yellow fever; the valleys of the Mississippi are subject to destructive inundations; the plains of the West are devastated by insects and drought, and our cities and country are swept by consuming fires. In all such cases, to gather and dispense the profuse liberality of our people, without waste of time or material, requires the wisdom that comes of experience and permanent organization. Still more does it concern, if not our safety, at least our honor, to signify our approval of those principles of humanity acknowledged by every other civilized nation.

# Paul Robeson

*"If we cannot as yet sing, 'Thank God Almighty, we're free at last,' we surely can all sing together: 'Thank God Almighty, we're moving!'"*

*Paul Robeson was one of the world's great interpretive artists. The son of an escaped slave became a true renaissance man — singer, actor, linguist, All-American football player, Rutgers University Phi Beta Kappa, and graduate of Columbia University Law School. In the late 1930s the stage and screen star became increasingly more outspoken on behalf of racial justice, social progress, and international peace. His motto, "The artist must elect to fight for freedom or slavery," epitomized his stand as he confronted President Harry Truman on antilynching legislation, fought to get black baseball players into the major leagues, and made countless speeches on behalf of labor, black, and peace groups — all of which made him a target of persecution during the McCarthy era and a virtual American boycott. In 1950, after he refused to sign Truman's "loyalty oath," the State Department revoked his passport. In the face of this onslaught Robeson redoubled his political activities. In 1939, after extensive travel abroad, Robeson made the following statement.*

I feel closer to my country than ever. There is no longer a feeling of lonesome isolation. Instead — peace. I return without fearing prejudice that once bothered me. It does not hurt or anger me now, for I know that people practice cruel bigotry in their ignorance, not maliciously. . . .

I've learned that my people are not the only ones oppressed. That it is the same for Jews or Chinese as for Negroes, and that such prejudice has no place in a democracy. I have sung my songs all over the world, and everywhere found that some common bond makes the people of all lands take to Negro songs, as to their own.

When I sang my American folk melodies in Budapest, Prague, Tiflis, Moscow, Oslo, the Hebrides, or the Spanish front, the people understood and wept or rejoiced with the spirit of the songs. I found that where forces have been the same, whether people weave, build, pick cotton, or dig in the mines, they understand each other in the common language of work, suffering, or protest. Their songs were composed by men trying to make work easier, trying to find a way out. . . .

Many of the old folk songs which are still young today echoed the terrific desire to escape bondage, such as the Negro protest song, "How long must my people weep and mourn." In Germany, today, when the oppressed commit suicide, or try to escape unbearable conditions, their actions cry out against the terrorized land they wish to leave. Our "Moses," with its "let my people go," never meant going to heaven — the direction was really north. Sojourner Truth, a Negro woman rebel who worked with John Brown in the liberation movement in the nineteenth century, used to sing this song as she passed through the woods to a Negro settlement; and when the Negroes heard it, they knew it was a signal for a meeting.

When I sing, "Let my people go," I can feel sympathetic vibrations from my audience, whatever its nationality. It is no longer just a Negro song — it is a symbol of those seeking freedom from the dungeons of fascism in Europe today. The same is true for the refugees with "Sometimes I feel like a motherless child a long way from home — Come my brother."

. . . This folk music is as much a creation of a mass people as language. Both are derived from social groups which had to communicate with each other and within each other. One person throws in a phrase. Then another — and when, as a singer, I walk from among the people, onto the people, to sing back to the people the songs they themselves have created, I can feel a great unity, not only as a person, but as an artist who is one with his audience. This keeping close to the feelings and desires of my audience has a lot to do with shaping my attitude toward the struggle of the people of the world. It has made me an antifascist, whether the struggle is in Spain, Germany, or here.

This, in turn, has made me see that the pseudo-scientific racial barriers which had been inculcated in me from cradle days upward were false. Even though I had won honors in university years, somehow these honors, instead of proving that color of skin made no difference, emphasized the difference all the more, since I was marked out as an exception to the rule.

The feeling that all this is wrong, a feeling which has come from my travels, from world events which show that all oppressed people cry out against their oppressors — these have made my loneliness vanish, have made me come home to sing my songs so that we will see that our democracy does not vanish. If I can contribute this as an artist, I shall be happy.

# Jane Addams

1860–1935

*"A settlement is an attempt to express the meaning of life in terms of life itself."*

*The name Jane Addams is synonymous with the words Hull House, the legendary settlement house she founded in Chicago in 1899. Addams worked out of Hull House and among its guests the remainder of her life, lobbying for such basic conditions as decent housing and fair labor practices for immigrants and the desperately poor. Responsible for such firsts as juvenile-court law, tenement-house regulation, an eight-hour work day for women, factory inspection, and worker's compensation, Addams's work marked the beginning of the Progressive movement in America. Under her leadership, an effort to overcome the dehumanizing effects of rapid industrialization through political, economic, and social reform took hold. A dedicated pacifist, Addams was president of the Women's International League for Peace and Freedom and was honored with the Nobel Peace Prize in 1931. Her words echoed l oudly as she lectured and published widely on the day's injustices and encouraged those called to social work.*

What is it that we would put before eager young people to make them feel the stir, and the pull, and the stress of this life in the city wilderness as something worthy of their steel, of their very finest endeavor? . . .

A young person possessed with a fine enthusiasm for a new social program may work side by side with the most careful social workers, who are also pushing it forward. But he must do it all with his feet on the ground. He must not do it from an a priori conception of what society might and ought to be. He must know his congested neighborhood and give reasons for the faith which is in him. He need not mount a box on the street corner and preach a new social order, but he must be able to say to the people about him, in regard to the tenement house which needs to be reconstructed and in regard to the street which needs to be cleaned, that he knows the best method of procedure in order to bring about these reforms. . . .

Forceful as is the student of sociology in the problems pressing for solution in the depressed quarters of the city, personally I have discovered that some of the best things are found and put forward by the man or woman who looks at life from this humanistic point of view. Such a young person sees the newly arrived immigrant, for instance, in relation to his past and to the things which his nationality and his race have brought to life; he tries to restore the immigrant to the framework from which he was torn when he came to America. The mind of such a young person nurtures and brings to fruit a certain beauty and culture and human development which would otherwise go to waste. But no one can undertake this humanistic task unless he is willing to bring the fruits of his own culture to bear upon the situation. So to any young person who wishes to go into the social field, I would say bring with you all that you can that softens life, all the poesy, all the sympathetic interpretation. You will need it all; and every scrap of history and language that you know, all of that which has made your own life rich, will be fairly torn off your back as you pass through those crowded city quarters.

Then there is the scientific mind that would apply to the old social problems of the household, to the care and nurture of children, to the prolongation of human life and the alleviation of old age, the scientific knowledge of our time. Thus far most of this valuable data has been lavished upon industries. Our factories estimate to a fraction the amount of power which a certain machine requires; they use every scrap of material, because waste is not only bad business but disgraceful; and when one goes into a tenement house quarter, one longs for a sign that such care is about to be bestowed upon the culture of human beings. . . . Why all this care for the product and so little concern for the producers? The businessman everywhere is using the best appliances that he may preserve his product and make it valuable. On the other side, what have we, the social workers, done for the producers? If we had the businessman's enthusiasm and his ability, if we had adequately asserted the claims of the producers, the community would have been obliged at length to recognize them. Let us not blame the businessman for his success, but see to it that he shall act as a spur to the rest of us. Will we belittle human fellowship by having it appear that business enterprise is more powerful? Our deepest morality says we must stand by the weak and the wretched and bring them into some sort of decency of life and social order.

# Wilma Mankiller

b. 1945

*"The Cherokee people care about competency and receiving services much more than whether there is a woman or a man leading the tribe."*

*In an historic tribal election in 1987, members of the Cherokee Nation of Oklahoma elected their first woman principal chief, Wilma Mankiller. In 1991 she was reelected with nearly 83 percent of the vote. During Mankiller's tenure as principal chief, tribal membership tripled in size and the annual budget doubled. Committed to rural community development and intent on redefining the quality of everyday life for her people, Mankiller initiated programs to improve health care, education, adult literacy, and utilities management. Chief Mankiller's success has resulted in an unprecedented worldwide interest in Native Americans that has enabled her to share the story of her tribe with the rest of the world. Intent on broadening her sphere of influence, she devotes her time to intergovernmental relations to bring about an enlightened congressional response to American Indian concerns. Shortly before celebrating a new generation of leaders, Mankiller related her optimism and trust in the Cherokee people.*

When I walked through the door of the Cherokee Nation offices in September of 1976 looking for a job, I never dreamed that I would someday have the honor and privilege of leading the second largest tribe in North America. I was a single mother of two children, and my primary focus was on how to support my children while making a contribution to the community. At that time, there were no female executives in the tribe; there had not been a female deputy chief or a female principal chief. The path to my eventual election as the deputy and later principal chief was not part of a strategy. Rather, it was the result of being in the right place at the right time, combined with my own willingness to take a risk. It has been said that I like to dance along the edge of a roof. I have never figured out whether that means I am self-confident or just impulsive. Either way, I was definitely out on the edge when I decided to run for elective office in my tribe.

None of the three elections was easy. Tribal politics, even in the best of circumstances, are much more personal and bruising than mainstream elective politics, in part because the electorate is like family. My being female made the elections that much more difficult.

Women learn to deal with overt gender-based opposition in different ways. In my case, I chose to ignore the opposition and remain focused on the issues at hand. I have been blessed with thick skin, for which I am very, very grateful. However, it was initially painful to have my own people not take me seriously because I am a woman or, even worse, ridicule my effort to become a leader in the Cherokee Nation.

In the old days, the Cherokee people believed that the world existed in a precarious balance and that only right or correct actions kept it from tumbling. Wrong actions were believed to disturb balance. In my view, gender balance in leadership is very important to all people. The viewpoint of men is important in all areas of society, as is the viewpoint of women. To ignore that balance and exclude from leadership an entire segment of society makes little sense in a time when we need the talents and skills of everyone to help grapple with the kind of problems we face each day. I am hopeful that I have been able to create an atmosphere in which the contributions of both women and men will be equally valued.

With the commitment and skills of a great staff and the support of the people, we have experienced exponential growth in virtually every area of the Cherokee Nation. Membership has increased during my tenure. Direct employment has doubled. The tribal budget has doubled to almost $90 million, and, most importantly, services to members have greatly expanded.

I am as hopeful and confident about the future of the Cherokee Nation as I was when I first began working here as an idealistic thirty-one-year-old woman. Fortunately, I have never overestimated my own significance to the Cherokee Nation. My tenure here will not even be a blip on the screen in the totality of Cherokee history. If there is any legacy I would like to leave, it would be that I did what I could during my fleeting time as leader of the great Cherokee Nation.

# Lee Iacocca

*"In the end your legacy is: Did you know what the hell you were doing?"*

*A forty-seven-year veteran of the automotive industry, Lee Iacocca is known as one of today's leading American executives — speaking out on subjects ranging from international industry to business ethics. After his much-publicized firing from the Ford Motor Company, where he introduced the best-selling Mustang, Iacocca was wedged in the public consciousness as the wonderboy of the failing Chrysler Corporation. Through layoffs, cutbacks, hard-selling advertising (including his personal "pitches"), and a guaranteed government loan, the "king of the minivan" restored Chrysler to profitability. He became the national model of a "will-do" executive who reduced business operations to three words: people, product, and profits. Feigning retirement, Iacocca continues to have an influence in the business community ("I'm still in demand as a public speaker because I'm good at it"), focusing on writing, fundraising, and investing. In his best-seller* Talking Straight, *he speaks to the next generation.*

In talking to students . . . [I] tell them to get mad. Because only angry people change things — people who get mad enough to say, "Wait a minute, I'm just not going to stand for this." While our young people have had their noses in their schoolbooks, we've been doing an absolutely miserable job of managing and moderating some of the violent economic changes taking place. My advice to them is to get mad about it. I don't mean riot in the streets. But get mad enough to demand the policies you need to compete in the world.

Get mad at the people in Washington who are burying you under a dungheap of debt. Tell them: "No more."

Get mad at the ideologues who want to make you martyrs to some eighteenth-century trade principles that everyone else ignores. Tell them: "I want a fair shot."

Get mad at anybody who tells you that you have to settle for packaged solutions. Tell them: "Get out of my way and let me think for myself."

That's how progress has always been made in this country of ours. People get mad and say, "That's enough!"

Americans have always been a practical people. Until lately, we've always put common sense ahead of ideology.

When you think about it, we don't even have a fundamental ideology in this country. The genius of the Constitution is its tolerance of so many points of view and espousal of none. I don't think that's an accident. The Founding Fathers were too smart to try to tell us how to solve our problems; they just gave us a framework to work in.

And so the Constitution is not a blueprint, like Karl Marx's *Manifesto* or Chairman Mao's *Little Red Book*. It doesn't tell us what our goals should be, or how to reach them. It simply lays out the powers of the government and then lists a few basic values that we're not allowed to mess around with — like freedom of speech, freedom of religion, freedom of assembly. Beyond that, we're on our own.

These rock-solid values — those basic freedoms — are really all you need. You can read the Constitution all day long and you won't find a single answer to the big problems we face today. There's nothing to tell you how to protect the environment, or what to do about terrorists, or how to put out a nuclear fire, or how to build the economy.

Which is just as well, because as Americans, we've often done a lousy job of figuring out just where we should be heading, but we've usually done a brilliant job of getting there. Why? Because we aren't visionaries — we're practical. And because we've held on to those basic values.

We aren't leaving our kids a blueprint to solve their problems, but then nobody gave us one either. And if they had, it wouldn't have worked. You see, such plans generally work only for the people who invent or devise them. Basically, we were on our own. And guess what? So are our kids. . . .

And so I hope that you who are our future leaders . . . keep asking yourselves that big question, and keep asking it over and over again: "What kind of America do I really want?" Up to now, you haven't had much of a choice. You've had to take the America that was handed to you. But now it's your turn.

Every generation of Americans has managed to leave the next one a little better off. That's part of our heritage. But each one leaves the next one a whole new set of challenges. And we sure are leaving you a couple of dandies!

# Zora Neale Hurston

1903–1960

*"Mama exhorted her children at every opportunity to 'jump at de sun.'*
*We might not land on the sun, but at least we would get off the ground."*

*Writer, anthropologist, and folklorist Zora Neale Hurston spent much of her life collecting the oral tradition of the South and other rural black communities. Her 1937 novel,* Their Eyes Were Watching God, *challenged her to present these folk stories authentically: the result was a fresh form of narrative fiction that housed a keen perspective on black life and an intimate portrayal of the human character. As the first African American to write a book of African-American folklore* (Mules and Men) *and one of the Harlem Renaissance's literati — Hurston termed the black literati the "niggerati" — she became as well known for her talent as for her brazen outspokenness, her distinct fashion, and her ownership of her black heritage. "I am not tragically colored," she said. Hurston died in poverty and remained relatively obscure, until the 1970s when her works were rediscovered by writer Alice Walker. The following is taken from Hurston's 1942 autobiography,* Dust Tracks on a Road.

There could be something wrong with me because I see Negroes neither better or worse than any other race. Race pride is a luxury I cannot afford. There are too many implications behind the term. Now, suppose a Negro does something really magnificent, and I glory, not in the benefit of mankind, but in the fact that the doer was a Negro. Must I not also go hang my head in shame when a member of my race does something execrable? If I glory, then the obligation is laid upon me to blush also. I do glory when a Negro does something fine, I gloat because he or she has done a fine thing, but not because he was a Negro. That is incidental and accidental. It is the human achievement which I honor. I execrate a foul act of a Negro but again not on the grounds that the doer was a Negro, but because it was foul. A member of my race just happened to be the fouler of humanity. In other words, I know that I cannot accept responsibility for 13 million people. Every tub must sit on its own bottom regardless. So "Race Pride" in me had to go. And anyway, why should I be proud to be a Negro? Why should anybody be proud to be white? Or yellow? Or red? After all, the word "race" is a loose classification of physical characteristics. It tells nothing about the insides of people. Pointing at achievements tells nothing either. Races have never done anything. What seems race achievement is the work of individuals. The white race did not go into a laboratory and invent incandescent light. That was Edison. The Jews did not work out Relativity. That was Einstein. The Negroes did not find out the inner secrets of peanuts and sweet potatoes, nor secret of the development of the egg. That was Carver and Just. If you are under the impression that every white man is an Edison, just look around a bit. If you have the idea that every Negro is a Carver, you had better take off plenty of time to do your searching.

No, instead of Race Pride being a virtue, it is a sapping vice. It has caused more suffering in the world than religious opinion, and that is saying a lot.

"Race Consciousness" is about the same as Race Pride in meaning. But, granting the shade of difference, all you say for it is, "Be continually conscious of what race you belong to so you can be proud." That is the effect of the thing. But what use is that? I don't care which race you belong to. If you are only one quarter honest in your judgment, you can seldom be proud. Why waste time keeping conscious of your physical aspects? What the world is crying and dying for at this moment is less race consciousness. The human race would blot itself out entirely if it had any more. It is a deadly explosive on the tongues of men. I choose to forget it.

# B e t t y   F o r d

b. 1918

*"I do not believe that being First Lady should prevent me from expressing my views. . . . Why should my husband's job or yours prevent us from being ourselves?"*

*In the aftermath of Watergate, Betty Ford was America's new First Lady, one who spoke her mind in support of the arts, physically challenged children, and women's issues, and worked ardently for the passage of the Equal Rights Amendment. In 1974, just weeks after moving into the White House, Ford faced the nation with an honest declaration: her diagnosis of breast cancer and impending mastectomy. By addressing an issue previously relegated to whispers and public service campaigns, she instantly raised the nation's conscience toward the disease and became an advocate for cancer awareness. Four years later, Ford admitted to her almost fifteen years of chemical dependency and began treatment. In 1982, she cofounded the Betty Ford Center in Rancho Mirage, California, regarded as the nation's premier alcohol and chemical dependency treatment center. In a speech penned for Cleveland's International Women's Year Congress, Ford presented thousands of women with words straight from the heart.*

I am here because I believe the best way to celebrate International Women's Year is to examine the very real problems women face today, not the progress of yesterday. While many new opportunities are open to women, too many are available only to the lucky few. Many barriers continue to block the paths of most women, even on the most basic issue of equal pay for equal work. And the contributions of women as wives and mothers continue to be underrated.

This year is not the time to cheer the visible few, but to work for the invisible many, whose lives are still restricted by custom and code. In working sessions of this conference, you will explore many of the formal and informal restrictions that confine women. Many of these restrictions spring directly from those emotional ideas about what women can and should do. These definitions of behavior and ability inhibit men and women alike, but the limits on women have been formalized into law and structured into social custom. For that reason, the first important steps have been to undo the laws that hem women and lock them out of the mainstream of opportunities.

But my own support of the Equal Rights Amendment has shown what happens when a definition of proper behavior collides with the right of an individual to personal opinions. I do not believe that being First Lady should prevent me from expressing my views. I spoke out on this important issue because of my deep personal convictions. Why should my husband's job or yours prevent us from being ourselves? Being ladylike does not require silence.

The Equal Rights Amendment when ratified will not be an instant solution to women's problems. It will not alter the basic fabric of the constitution — or force women away from their families. It will help knock down those restrictions that have locked women in old stereotypes of behavior and opportunity. It will help open up more options for women. But it is only a beginning.

The debate over the ERA has become too emotional, because of the fears of some — both men and women — about the changes already taking place in America. And part of the job of those who support the ERA is to help remove this cloud of fear and confusion. Change by its very nature is threatening, but it is also often productive. And the fight of women to become more productive, accepted human beings is important to all people of either sex or whatever nationality. I hope that 1976 will be the year the remaining four states ratify the Twenty-seventh Amendment. It will be an important symbolic event during our 200th birthday to show that the great American experiment in human freedom continues to expand.

But changing laws, more job opportunities, less financial discrimination, and more possibilities for the use of our minds and bodies will only partially change the place of American women. By themselves they will never be enough, because we must value our own talents before we can expect acceptance from others. The heart of the battle is within. . . .

Freedom for women to be what they want to be will help complete the circle of freedom America has been striving for during two hundred years. As the barriers against freedom for Americans because of race or religion have fallen, the freedom of all has expanded. The search for human freedom can never be complete without freedom for women. By the end of this century, I hope this nation will be a place where men and women can freely choose their life's work without restrictions or without ridicule. On the eve of this nation's third century, let us work to end the laws and remove the labels that limit the imaginations and the options of men and women alike.

# Benjamin Spock

1903–1998

*"I believe that the key to a better world for our children — and ourselves — is to reassert the importance of values and to encourage idealism."*

*Pediatrician, psychiatrist, author, and social activist, Benjamin Spock became known universally as "Dr. Spock" when in 1946 he published* The Common Sense Book of Baby and Child Care. *His best-seller status (with millions of copies sold) made him both the hero and villain of late-twentieth-century American child rearing — his flexible approach was regarded by many as humane and others as excessively permissive. In the 1960s, the nation's "friendly baby doctor" became increasingly known for his pacifism, opposing the Vietnam War under the conviction, "What is the use of physicians like myself trying to help parents bring up children healthy and happy, to have them killed in such numbers for a cause that is ignoble?" After a brief run for the presidency Dr. Spock spent much of the next quarter-century living on and sailing boats, pausing to send monthly letters to his congressmen supporting nuclear disarmament and endorsing the recent claim that cows' milk harms children.*

Anthropological studies from all over the world, to say nothing of the historical record, show that children can be taught any set of values that their parents and their group truly believe in. If children worship material success rather than truth or compassion, it is only because they have absorbed those values from others. To counteract this, it is not enough merely to preach to them. If parents preach morality to their children but behave hypocritically, the children are more likely to become cynics than saints. Instead, parents must hold to a set of values and maintain their own idealism, so that their children will be inspired by their example. . . . I too believe that our society has misplaced its values and lost its bearings. However, I believe that the solution is not to rush backward, eyes closed, groping for the answers of the past, but instead to look for the causes of our problems and for realistic solutions that might fit those causes. I believe there are at least three major reasons why so many people in our society have lost their belief in themselves and in the values closest to their hearts.

Christian, Jewish, and Muslim religions teach that human beings were created in God's image and for God's purposes. This teaching has traditionally given people a strong sense of purpose and dignity. But the steady expansion of scientific knowledge in the last two centuries — particularly in biology, anthropology, and psychology — has undermined the biblical explanation of the world, of humanity's place in it, and of humanity's special relationship to God. The gradual acceptance of humanity's having a less exalted place in the overall scheme of things has, I believe, had a profound and depressing effect. It has deflated our spirits, but so slowly that most of us do not recognize how or when it happened.

As valuable as biology, anthropology, and psychology are to understanding our human existence, each recognizes only a limited and rather mechanical aspect of humanity. The complexity of the human being is left out, particularly the spiritual and idealistic aspects that differentiate us most from other animals — those aspects once called the soul. This omission has led many people to the cynical conclusion that we should stop worrying about any higher aspirations and settle for enjoyment of our lower, animal nature.

A third reason for our rejection of the standards of the past has been our protest — conscious and unconscious — against the excessive artificiality of the nineteenth century: the overly proper Victorian manners, the denial of our negative emotions, the suppression of sexuality, the emphasis on making a good appearance at any cost. It seems to me that in our degrading language, our tattered clothes, our emphasis on the physical aspects of sexuality we are still, after a hundred years, rebelling against the pomposity and stuffy propriety of our Victorian ancestors.

As powerful as these reasons are, however, I believe we can and should challenge them. Unless a substantial proportion of people hold to positive standards, beliefs, and ideals, a society begins to come apart at the seams. We are seeing it happen: materialism unchecked by idealism leads to oppression of the powerless by the greedy; excessive competitiveness hardens hearts even within families; tolerance of violence unleashes all sorts of brutality; acceptance of instability in marriage encourages ever greater instability; the absence of values in children leads to a generation of cynical, self-centered adults. I believe that spiritual values and idealism — within or without organized religion — are as real and as powerful as the physical and intellectual attributes of [a] human being. I believe that we can give our children standards to live by and keep them from cynically accepting amorality and immorality, even though much of society as a whole may be corrupt and cynical.

# Sally Ride

b. 1951

*"It's time that people realize that women in this country can do any job that they want to do."*

*At twenty-seven years old, Sally Ride was a Ph.D. candidate looking for postdoctoral work in astrophysics when she heard about NASA's call for astronauts. More than eight thousand men and women applied to the space program; Ride was one of only six women accepted. On June 27, 1983, Ride became the first American woman space traveler when she was launched aboard the* Challenger STS-7. *Just over a year later she boarded the* Challenger *again, this time for an historic eight-day flight. Dr. Ride moved to NASA Headquarters in Washington where she became assistant to the NASA administrator for long-range planning and created NASA's Office of Exploration. Currently a professor of physics at the University of California at San Diego, Dr. Ride encourages young women to study science and math and meet their own* Challenger *destinies. She presented the following thoughts about her role as the first woman in space at the STS-7 preflight crew press conference.*

I didn't come into this program to be the first woman in space. I came in to get a chance to fly as soon as I could, and I'm planning to stay in it as long as they'll let me.

I have come to realize that I will be a role model. That's something that I didn't come to NASA intending to be, that's not why I joined the program, you know. I joined the program to get a chance to fly. And I guess that as far as being a role model is concerned, what I intend to do is just do what I've been trained to do, do as good of a job as I can while I'm up there, and hope that that provides a good role model. . . .

I think that NASA has really done me a great favor by allowing me to continue training to the extent that I needed to train during last year. And they filtered all the interview requests that came in, and really made sure I wasn't spending time, that I should have been spending training, doing interviews. And as a result of that, I really haven't felt much pressure, and I haven't felt that it's cutting into my training time at all. And I'm really grateful that NASA took that approach in leading up to this flight. Because I think that it would have been doing me a disservice and probably doing NASA a disservice to take away from the training time to do interviews before the flight. . . .

It's too bad that our society isn't further along, and that [being the first American woman in space] is such a big deal. But I guess if the American public thinks that it's a big deal, then it's probably good that it's getting the coverage it's getting. I think it's time we get away from that, and it's time that people realize that women in this country can do any job that they want to do.

# B i l l   G a t e s

b. 1955

*"The twentieth century has been the American Century in large part because of great inventors like the Wright brothers. May we follow their flight paths and blaze our own."*

*Bill Gates's vision for personal computing revolutionized the way that people relate to machines. As the chairman and CEO of Microsoft Corporation — a company he dropped out of Harvard to start — Gates transformed American homes and businesses with the development of his DOS operating system, which became the dominant operating system in America when IBM adopted it for its line of personal computers in the early 1980s. Microsoft's vision of a "computer on every desk and in every home" is coupled today with a commitment to Internet-related technologies that expand the power of the PC and its users. In the dozen years since Microsoft went public, Gates has donated more than $800 million to charities, including more than $200 million to help libraries take advantage of the information age. In 1996 he wrote the following essay regarding freedom of speech on the Internet and his concerns about legislation that would impose inappropriate constraints on freedom of speech.*

The Internet is the first medium that allows anyone with reasonably inexpensive equipment to publish to a wide audience. It is the first medium that distributes information globally at almost no marginal cost. The Internet's potential is enormous, and the stakes are high. The Internet can raise the quality of political debate, the quality of education, the quality of life. It is precious and important, and we must not take it for granted.

Beginning two decades ago, the PC industry developed in the United States without government control and regulations. The benefits of the resulting PC revolution were far-reaching.

As this computer revolution gives way to an even-more-important communication revolution, governments are getting involved — sometimes with a vengeance.

One example of government involvement is the telecommunications-deregulation bill that President Bill Clinton recently signed into law. It will, among other things, make the "information highway" of the future possible.

Overall, Microsoft and I supported this legislation, in part because it will help create a framework that will encourage aggressive private investment. The result will be faster communications connections and lower costs for people who use interactive networks such as the Internet. This will be good for our economy and way of life.

But not everything about the bill is good. In fact, one part is truly bad.

Microsoft and others in industry and nonprofit organizations were deeply involved in trying to block language that would put chilling restrictions on the use of the Internet for the free publication of information. The language, ostensibly aimed at keeping pornography out of the hands of children, goes much too far in restricting freedom of expression.

We had a lot of good company in the fight against this knee-jerk language, but we lost the first round.

Now our hope is that this misguided language will either be struck down by the courts as unconstitutional or else overridden legislatively.

If it is allowed to stand, it will undermine our nation's Bill of Rights — and there is no question that it will interfere with the ability of the Internet to flourish. It is so restrictive that it will scare people who fear they might commit a felony, by simply discussing a controversial topic.

We in the United States have a heartfelt interest in keeping pornography and other objectionable material out of the hands of children. We can't turn our heads and ignore that which can damage our kids.

But we also have a national interest in freedom of expression. Throughout history, that freedom has been a hallmark of our nation which has benefited our society, and helped us set an example for the world.

The free exchange of ideas on a global basis is something that is important for the U.S. politically and economically. Let's not undermine the worldwide trend toward free expression by setting a bad example when it comes to free speech on a computer network.

The Bill of Rights is the foundation on which our nation is built. The Internet is an enormously valuable place in which those rights must continue to thrive. Both the Bill of Rights and the Internet are potentially fragile. Mess with either of them too much, and we might ruin them.

We can't let this happen.

# Clare Boothe Luce

**1903–1987**

*"A large, unmeasurable percentage of the total editorial space in American newspapers is concerned not with public affairs or matters of stately importance. It is devoted instead to entertainment, titillation, amusement, voyeurism, and tripe."*

*Intelligent and controversial are just two words that describe legendary playwright, journalist, and politician Clare Boothe Luce. She was also determined and tenacious. Her credits include editorial posts at* Vogue *and* Vanity Fair *and playwright credits for several Broadway hits, including* The Women, *which Luce penned in three days. Seldom celebrated are her years of wartime journalism as World War II news correspondent for* Life, *a magazine she conceived with her husband-publisher magnate Henry R. Luce. Her encounter with the war produced her first nonfiction work,* Europe in the Spring. *Luce entered politics in the 1940s, first as a Republican congresswoman, and then as the first woman diplomat to a foreign country when, in 1953, President Dwight D. Eisenhower appointed her ambassador to Italy. In her quest for definition as a woman "first," Luce drew on her acerbic wit and charm, evident here in her address to journalists during a Women's National Press Club event.*

It is easy to point out many instances in which the American press — especially its individual members — tend to abuse their freedom and shirk their responsibility. For example, one could note that nowadays the banner of press freedom is more often raised in matters of printing crime, sex, and scandal stories than it is in matters of printing truth about great national figures, policies, and issues. Or that too many members of the working press uncritically pass on — even if they do not personally swallow — too much high-level government and political cant, tripe, and public relations; or that there are too many journalists who seem willing to sell their birthright of candor and truth in order to become White House pets, party pets, corporation pets, Pentagon or State Department or trade union or governor's mansions pets; who wistfully yearn after gray eminency, or blatantly strive for publicity for themselves, or lecture platforms or political rostrums.

While agreeing with most journalists that people are not as much interested in the issues as they could be, one could note that neither are many journalists. One could mention that such journalists seem to have forgotten that men, not names alone, make news, and that men are made by the clarity with which they state issues, and the resolution with which they face them. One could express the hope that more journalists would encourage rather than avoid controversy and argument, remembering that controversy and argument are not the enemies of democracy but its friends. One could wish for fewer journalist prodigies of well-written factual story, and more gifted talents for drawing explanations from the facts, or that working pressmen would be more creative in reporting the news, or that they would reflect less in themselves of what in this decade they have so roundly condemned in American leadership: apathy, criticism, lukewarmness, and acceptance as the status quo about everything, from juvenile delinquency to nuclear destruction. One could pray, above all, for journalists who cared less about ideologies and more about ideas. . . .

The double charge against the American press may be stated: its failure to inform the public better than it does is the evasion of its responsibility; its failure to educate and elevate the public taste rather than following that taste like a blind, wallowing dinosaur is an abuse of its freedom. In the view of the river of information which flows daily from the typewriters of American correspondents, why are the American people not better informed? Whose fault is it? At first glance it would seem to be the fault of the publishers, and especially editors. But the publisher or editor who does not give his readers plenty of what they want is going to lose circulation to a competitor who does. Or if he has a news monopoly in his city, and feels too free to shortchange them on these things, he is going to lose circulation as his reader slack is taken up by the radio, the TV, and the magazines. . . .

Can we quarrel with this? We cannot. The Declaration of Independence itself set the pattern of the American way, and with it American reading habits. Life, liberty, and the pursuit of happiness were to be man's prime and legitimate goals. Perhaps the history of our country would have been better — and happier — if "the pursuit of truth, information, and enlightenment" had been his third great goal. But that was not the way our founding fathers saw things. And that is not the way the American public sees them now. Today, as yesterday, people are primarily moved in their choice of reading by their daily emotions, their personal, immediate, existential prejudices, biases, ambitions, desires, and — as we know too well in the Freudian age — by many subconscious yearnings and desires, and irrational hates and fears. Very well then: let us accept the fact. Should the American press bow to it? Accept it? Cater to it? Foster it? What else (the cynical and sophisticated will ask) is there to do?

# J o d y   W i l l i a m s

**b. 1950**

*"Ordinary people can achieve extraordinary things — but only if they take action. Emotion without action is wasted."*

*Corecipient of the 1997 Nobel Peace Prize, human rights activist Jody Williams is the founding coordinator of the International Campaign to Ban Landmines (ICBL), which was formally launched by six nongovernmental organizations in October 1992. In only six years, Williams, who served as the chief strategist and spokesperson for the campaign, oversaw the growth of the ICBL to more than one thousand nongovernmental organizations in more than seventy-five countries. Working in an unprecedented cooperative effort with governments, United Nations bodies, and the International Committee of the Red Cross, the ICBL achieved its goal of an international treaty banning landmines in September 1997. At the time of print, 135 nations had signed the treaty. Although several countries have not yet signed, including the United States, Williams believes they will. Williams, who now serves as an "ambassador" for the ICBL, speaks on her life mission.*

People often ask how I became involved in this global effort to ban landmines. One answer is simple: I was asked to put together a coalition of nongovernmental organizations to pressure governments to negotiate a treaty to get rid of this insidious weapon — and I agreed. Another is more complicated and is part of the question that one can ask anyone about themselves: How did you turn out the way you are? Why do you do what you do?

Like many of my generation, the Vietnam War was a defining experience for me, one that made me question authority and begin to understand the conflicts between U.S. "ideals" and its policies that often fly in the face of those ideals. At the time, I had no idea how much Vietnam would influence the course of my life.

Also like many of my generation, I didn't really know what to do with my liberal arts degree after graduating, so I went back to school! After receiving my master's, I lived in Mexico and taught English as a second language. That experience gave me a new understanding of class differences, with gross disparities between the rich and the poor, which so often are root causes of armed conflict.

A couple of years later, these experiences came together in a single moment at a subway stop in Washington, D.C., where I was handed a leaflet entitled, "El Salvador: Another Vietnam?" It resonated for me instantly and deeply — deeply enough that I went to a meeting in a church basement to learn about the wars in Central America. And there I met Mario Velasquez, a political spokesperson for the FMLN, El Salvador's guerilla movement, and immediately began working to change U.S. policy toward Central America.

The twists of fate are strange sometimes. If that leaflet had not mentioned Vietnam it is very likely that I would not have gone to that church that night. But it did and I didn't want to see this country go down the road again to disrupting the lives of a tiny, tiny part of the world that it seemed to know nothing about. And the passion of doing what I considered to be the right thing captured me, and I've never looked back. I worked for over a decade to stop the wars in Central America. I was still doing it when I was asked to help launch the landmine campaign.

The work to ban landmines is, in part, a human rights issue. Landmines are called eternal sentinels because they kill civilians and disrupt aid efforts long after a war is over. In most of the armed conflicts of the recent decades, fighting forces have put landmines where people live and work — on purpose, to disrupt normal life and terrorize civilian populations. Twenty-six thousand people, most of them civilians and many of them children, are killed or maimed each year by landmines. But people who were aware of this long-term impact of the weapon decided that the time had come to do something about them.

I just happened to be one of those people. I am now forty-eight years old and my work has been recognized with the Nobel Peace Prize. Yet I'm still wondering what I'm going to do with the rest of my life. Now I have a whole new set of pressures and expectations, partly because of the Nobel Laureate label, and partly because I'm only the third American woman to ever receive the prize. People expect me to be a certain way. That's great, but I am still Jody Williams and I still need to do what is right for me. The only thing I know is that I still, every single day of my life, get up with joy and excitement and wonder about what I'm going to do today to try to make a difference in the world.

# Martin Luther King Jr.

**1929–1968**

*"The old law of an eye for an eye leaves everybody blind."*

*It is impossible to separate the words, wisdom, and dreams of Dr. Martin Luther King Jr. from the fabric of American life. His advocacy of equality and the marches he led shaped thirteen years of civil rights activities; his concept of "some-bodiness" gave black and poor people a new sense of worth and dignity; his philosophy of nonviolent social action and his strategies for nondestructive change sparked the conscience of the nation. In early 1963, thousands of black citizens were being turned away as they tried to register to vote in Mississippi, and downtown Birmingham, Alabama, remained segregated. "Civil rights," wrote the Nobel Peace Prize winner, "no longer commanded the conscience of the nation." King's peace march from Montgomery, Alabama, to Birmingham that year established his commitment to nonviolence — and landed him in jail. On April 16, 1963, from the depths of solitary confinement, King wrote his epic "Letter from Birmingham Jail."*

We know through painful experience that freedom is never voluntarily given by the oppressor; it must be demanded by the oppressed. Frankly, I have never yet engaged in a direct action movement that was "well timed," according to the timetable of those who have not suffered unduly from the disease of segregation.

For years now I have heard the words [sic] "Wait!" It rings in the ear of every Negro with a piercing familiarity. This "Wait" has almost always meant "Never." We must come to see with the distinguished jurist of yesterday that "justice too long delayed is justice denied."

We have waited for more than 340 years for our constitutional and God-given rights. The nations of Asia and Africa are moving with jetlike speed toward the goal of political independence, and we still creep at horse and buggy pace toward the gaining of a cup of coffee at a lunch counter.

I guess it is easy for those who have never felt the stinging darts of segregation to say, "Wait." But when you have seen vicious mobs lynch your mothers and fathers at will and drown your sisters and brothers at whim; when you have seen hate-filled policemen curse, kick, brutalize and even kill your black brothers and sisters with impunity;

when you see the vast majority of your 20 million Negro brothers smothering in an airtight cage of poverty in the midst of an affluent society; when you suddenly find your tongue twisted and your speech stammering as you seek to explain to your six-year-old daughter why she can't go to the public amusement park that has just been advertised on television, and see tears welling up in her eyes when she is told that Funtown is closed to colored children, and see the depressing clouds of inferiority begin to form in her little mental sky, and see her begin to distort her little personality by unconsciously developing a bitterness toward white people;

when you have to concoct an answer for a five-year-old son asking in agonizing pathos: "Daddy, why do white people treat colored people so mean?"; when you take a cross-country drive and find it necessary to sleep night after night in the uncomfortable corners of your automobile because no motel will accept you; when you are humiliated day in and day out by nagging signs reading "white" and "colored";

when your first name becomes "nigger," your middle name becomes "boy" (however old you are), and your last name becomes "John," and your wife and mother are never given the respected title "Mrs."; when you are harried by day and haunted by night by the fact that you are a Negro, living constantly at tiptoe stance never quite knowing what to expect next, and plagued with inner fears and outer resentments; when you are forever fighting a degenerating sense of "nobodiness"; then you will understand why we find it difficult to wait.

# Katharine Hepburn

b. 1907

*"In some ways, I've had it all. I don't know about the life I didn't have because I didn't choose it. I can't regret a life I didn't choose."*

*Critics and fans alike deem Katharine Hepburn the most distinguished, durable, and individualistic actress in film history. The daughter of a suffragette, Hepburn owes her autonomy to her family's liberal interpretation of gender roles, a theme she carried into celluloid and onto Broadway. Portraying atypical characters from tomboys to fashion divas, Hepburn is the first woman to win three best actress Oscars — for* Morning Glory, Guess Who's Coming to Dinner, *and* The Lion in Winter. *She received another Oscar for* On Golden Pond, *making her the only performer to capture four Academy Awards. Priding herself for becoming the antithesis of wife and mother, Hepburn never hesitated to take controversial stands for the Equal Rights Amendment and birth control. "I put on pants fifty years ago," the legend said at seventy-two. "I have not lived as a woman. I have lived as a man. I've just done what I damn well wanted to."*

The only hold I've ever had on an audience that I felt was valid was that, in a curious way, from the time I was little, I understood instinctively the misgivings of the human race — the doubts, the fears, and I could see through the bluffs. And when I played to an audience, I tried deliberately to present what I thought was elevating in the human being — which I think human beings automatically reach for. People have told me how much this has meant to them. Otherwise, wouldn't they say, "God damn her, she's had everything . . ."?

The thing is, I just don't like to be half-good. It drives me crazy to be mediocre — just drives me insane. And I'm willing to do anything to try to be really good. I'm very aware when I'm very good — and I like to be very, very good. Oh, I think perfection is the only standard for people who are stars. . . .

Professionalism is a word I don't like. It's rather flat, indicates a lack of inspiration. It sounds automatic, and it never should be. That's the great danger in the business. You can be too-too-too whatever you are, all the sort of things you're known for. And the danger is that you will do it automatically.

Movies have changed so much. They call movies honest because they can use every word and can photograph people rolling around and carrying on in an idiotic way. They're not honest at all! To photograph love! You can't do that, can you? And friendship, you can't photograph that. Not that way. If you underplay it and use your imagination, the audience will do all the acting for you. I don't have to leap on you and groan and carry on, you know! I mean, surely, they can get the message, can't they? What do you think has happened to our taste? It's agony. . . .

We are enormously impressed by success because there's so much failure. The margin of difference is often so tiny. Everyone has a breaking point that defeats and destroys them. Luckily I haven't met mine yet. But then I've always had a place to turn and a home waiting; so I don't give myself too much credit. I was fired lots of times but I was never fired when I was in the middle of the East River swimming for shore with the current against me. Even when things were going badly for me, I still turned down all kinds of offers because I didn't like them. I never had to say yes when I wanted to say no. I used to say, "Hell, I don't want to drown in somebody else's dress." If people can just keep going beyond a certain point then they're great. But you see people trying to constantly reach that level and just as they're about to be able to pull themselves onto the dock and sit down — they drown. And you must not let yourself drown.

# Acknowledgments

*An undertaking of historical perspective and content requires the assistance of many dedicated people.*

For their encouragement and support, I would like to thank my team at New World Library: Marc Allen, Becky Benenate, Cathy Bodenmann, Dean Campbell, Victoria Clarke, Marjorie Conte, Jason Gardner, Amy Garretson, Munro Magruder, Ryan Madden, and Tona Pearce Myers. A special thank you is reserved for Mary Ann Casler, for her superb design skills and production efforts. Thanks are also due to Chris Cone and Judy Reeves, whose sharp editorial eye enhanced the words on the page, and to Todd Anderson, Sara Dunn, and Victor Perry, for their research skills.

Over the course of editing the book, many featured heroes and their support staff spoke encouragingly of the concept and were particularly gracious with their time and resources. I would like to thank Josephine Chaplin, Penny Cook, Lori de Leon, Elisabeth Edwards, Rebecca Fishkin, Gary Gailor, Kate Guyonvarch, Dolores Huerta, Stan Jackson, Sue A. Leary, Dr. William and Kathleen Magee, Wilma Mankiller, Gina Olaya-Quinton, Elizabeth Reynolds, Amy Richards, Gloria Steinem, Toby White, and Jody Williams. I salute all the contributors who willingly shared their lives — without their messages there would be no book.

I'd also like to acknowledge the photographers, whose work speaks for itself, including Russ Busby, Michael Collopy, Ching-Ming Cheung, Julie Jensen, Bill Miles, Gene Pushkar, Hulleah J. Tsinhnahjinnie, and Jenny Warburg.

Reference librarians, museum staff, university personnel, and other benevolent folk met demanding research requests that challenged them to put their patience to work. The following deserve credit for going above and beyond the call of duty: Ann Barbaro, Evelyn Benjamin, Amy Boardley, John Boop, Ann Bremner, Gabrielle Bresnik, Woodfin Camp, Dina Carter, Wendy Chmielewski, Brian DeShazor, Steve Garber, David Gold, Barbara Hill, Charlotte Holliman, Pheobe Jacobs, Brooke Kroeger, Donna Lehman, David Loehr, Nancy Mirshah, David Newell, Hedda Sharapan, Suzanne Smailes, Netzin and Maxine Steklis, and Rick Wyman.

Finally, I would like to thank my family for their strength and encouragement in the face of many deadlines. Their generosity made writing time possible.

# Permissions Acknowledgments

Grateful acknowledgment is given to the following for permission to reprint the photography and text excerpts in *Imagine*:

Jane Addams: Photo courtesy of Jane Addams Collection, Swarthmore College Peace Collection. Excerpt reprinted with permission of Simon & Schuster from *Twenty Years at Hull House* by Jane Addams. © 1910 by Macmillan Publishing Company, renewed 1938 by James W. Linn.

Madeleine Albright: Photo courtesy of U.S. State Department.

Muhammad Ali: Photo courtesy of CORBIS/Michael Brennan. Excerpt reprinted with permission of Simon & Schuster, Inc. from *Muhammad Ali: His Life and Times* by Thomas Hauser. © 1991 by Thomas Hauser and Muhammad Ali.

Susan B. Anthony: Photo courtesy of Huntington Library/SuperStock. Excerpt courtesy of the Library of Congress, Susan B. Anthony Papers.

Louis Armstrong: Photo courtesy of CORBIS/Hulton-Deutsch Collection. Excerpt courtesy Richard Meryman/*Life* magazine. © Time Inc. Reprinted by permission of Time Life Syndication and the estate of Louis Armstrong.

Neil Armstrong: Photo © NASA. Excerpt from NASA press conference transcripts, courtesy of NASA Historical Archives. Reprinted by permission.

Lucille Ball: Photo and essay © Lucille Ball Productions, Inc., and Desilu, too, LLC. All rights reserved. Reprinted with permission.

Clara Barton: Photo courtesy of CORBIS.

Nellie Bly: Photo courtesy of CORBIS/Bettmann.

Margaret Bourke-White: Photo courtesy of *Life* magazine. © Time Inc. Reprinted by permission of Time Inc. Excerpt reprinted by permission of the estate of Margaret Bourke-White.

Rachel Carson: Photo courtesy of CORBIS/Underwood & Underwood. Excerpt from *Silent Spring* by Rachel Carson. © 1962 by Rachel L. Carson. © renewed 1990 by Roger Christie. Reprinted by permission of Houghton Mifflin Company. All rights reserved.

Charlie Chaplin: Photo courtesy of SuperStock. Dialogue from *The Great Dictator* © Roy Export Company Establishment. Reprinted by permission of the Association Chaplin.

Hillary Clinton: Photo courtesy of the White House.

James Dean: Photo courtesy of the David Loehr Collection. Reprinted by permission of David Loehr and the James Dean Memorial Gallery.

Amelia Earhart: Photo © 1937 Albert Bresnick. Reprinted by permission of Gabrielle Bresnick. Excerpt courtesy of *Aero News and Mechanics*.

Thomas Edison: Photo courtesy of Stock Montage/SuperStock.

Marian Wright Edelman: Photo © Michael Callopy. Stand for Children Day speech © 1996 Children's Defense Fund. Excerpt and photo reprinted by permission of the Children's Defense Fund.

Albert Einstein: Photo © Yousuf Karsh. Courtesy of Woodfin Camp & Associates, Inc. Excerpt from *The World As I See It* copyright by the Albert Einstein Archives. Reprinted by permission of The Hebrew University of Jerusalem, Israel.

William Faulkner: Photo courtesy of CORBIS/Bettmann. Excerpt from *Essays, Speeches, and Public Letters by William Faulkner*, edited by James P. Meriwether. © 1950 by William Faulkner. Reprinted by permission of Random House, Inc.

Ella Fitzgerald: Photo courtesy of CORBIS/Hulton-Deutsch Collection. "A-Tisket A-tasket" by Ella Fitzgerald and Van Alexander. © 1938 (Renewed) EMI Robbins Catalog Inc. All rights reserved. Used by permission. Warner Bros. Publications U.S. Inc., Miami, FL 33014.

Betty Ford: Photo © Yousuf Karsh. Courtesy of Woodfin Camp & Associates, Inc.

Henry Ford: Photo courtesy of CORBIS.

Dian Fossey: Photo © and courtesy of the Dian Fossey Gorilla Fund International, 800 Cherokee Avenue SE, Atlanta, Georgia, 30315; (800) 851-0202; www.gorillafund.org. Used by permission. Excerpt from *Gorillas in the Mist*. © 1983 by Dian Fossey. Reprinted by permission of Houghton Mifflin Company. All rights reserved.

Bill Gates: Photo courtesy of CORBIS/Lynn Goldsmith. Excerpt © 1999 Microsoft Corporation, One Microsoft Way, Redmond, Washington, 98052-6399, U.S.A. All rights reserved. Reprinted with permission from Microsoft Corporation.

Billy Graham: Photo courtesy of the Billy Graham Evangelistic Association. Excerpt © 1996 Billy Graham Evangelistic Association. Used by permission, all rights reserved.

Martha Graham: Photo courtesy of CORBIS. Excerpt from *Blood Memory* by Martha Graham. © 1997 by Martha Graham. Used by permission of Doubleday, a division of Random House, Inc.

Jim Henson: Photo courtesy of CORBIS/Bettmann. Excerpt from *Jim Henson: The Works,* edited by Christopher Finch. © 1993 by Jim Henson Productions, Inc. Reprinted by permission of Random House.

Katharine Hepburn: Photo courtesy of CORBIS/Bettmann. Excerpt courtesy of *Ladies' Home Journal*.

David Ho: Photo and excerpt reprinted by permission of Dr. David Ho and the Aaron Diamond AIDS Research Center.

Dolores Huerta: Photo © 1999 Idaljiza Liz-Lepriorz. Excerpt courtesy of Pacifica Radio Archives, North Hollywood, California, and reprinted by permission of Pacifica Radio Archives and Dolores Huerta.

Zora Neale Hurston: Photo courtesy of CORBIS. Excerpt from appendix "Seeing the World As It Is" from *Dust Tracks on a Road* by Zora Neale Hurston. © 1942 by Zora Neale Hurston. Copyright renewed 1970 by John C. Hurston. Reprinted by permission of HarperCollins Publishers, Inc.

Lee Iacocca: Photo © Wally McNamee. Courtesy of Woodfin Camp & Associates, Inc. Excerpt from *Talking Straight* by Lee Iacocca. © 1988 by Lee Iacocca. Used by permission of Bantam Books, a division of Random House, Inc.

Magic Johnson: Photo courtesy of CORBIS/Neal Preston. Excerpt from *My Life* by Earvin "Magic" Johnson. © 1992 by June Bug Enterprises. Reprinted by permission of Random House, Inc.

Helen Keller: Photo © Yousuf Karsh. Courtesy of Woodfin Camp & Associates, Inc. Excerpt courtesy of the American Foundation for the Blind. Reprinted by permission.

John F. Kennedy: Photo courtesy of CORBIS.

Martin Luther King Jr: Photo courtesy of CORBIS/Flip Schulke. Excerpt © 1963 by Martin Luther King Jr., © renewed 1991 by Coretta Scott King. Reprinted by arrangement with the Heirs to the Estate of Martin Luther King Jr., c/o Writer's House, Inc. as agent for the proprietor.

Maggie Kuhn: Photo © Julie Jensen. Excerpt reprinted by permission of the estate of Maggie Kuhn.

John Lennon: Photo courtesy of CORBIS/Hulton-Deutsch Collection. "Imagine" words and music by John Lennon. © 1971 Lenono Music. All rights controlled and administered by EMI Blackwood Music Inc. All rights reserved. International copyright secured. Used with permission.

Maya Lin: Photo © Ching-Ming Cheung. Excerpt from "Conversation with Maya Lin," an interview with Sarah J. Rogers, in the exhibition catalogue *Maya Lin: Public Private*. Columbus, Ohio: Wexner Center for the Arts, The Ohio State University, 1994. Reprinted with permission.

Clare Boothe Luce: Photo courtesy of CORBIS. Excerpt reprinted by permission of the Henry Luce Foundation, Inc.

William and Kathleen Magee: Photo © Bill Miles. Excerpt © 1999 by William and Kathleen Magee. Reprinted by permission of Operation Smile.

Wilma Mankiller: Photo courtesy of Hulleah J. Tsinhnahjinnie. Excerpt reprinted by permission of Wilma Mankiller.

Margaret Mead: Photo © Ken Heymen. Courtesy of Woodfin Camp & Associates, Inc. Excerpt from *Margaret Mead: Some Personal Views*. © 1979 by Mary Catherine Bateson and Rhoda Metraux. Reprinted by permission of Walker and Company, 435 Hudson Street, New York, NY 10014. All rights reserved.

Grandma Moses: Photo of Grandma Moses in her hundredth year. © 1999 Grandma Moses Properties, New York. Photo by Hildegard Bachert. Excerpt from *My Life's History*, by Grandma Moses. Reprinted by permission of Grandma Moses Properties.

Georgia O'Keeffe: Photo by Carl Van Vechten. Forms part of the Carl Van Vechten Photo Collection (Library of Congress). Excerpt from the catalogue *Exhibition of Oils and Pastels: January 22–March 17, 1939*. Courtesy of the Beinecke Rare Book and Manuscript Library, Yale University. Reprinted by permission of the Georgia O'Keeffe Foundation.

Rosa Parks: Photo courtesy of CORBIS/Bettman. Excerpt taken from *Quiet Strength* by Rosa Parks with Gregory J. Reed. © 1995 by Rosa Parks. Used by permission of Zondervan Publishing House.

Sally Ride: Photo courtesy of CORBIS/Bettman. Excerpt from the STS-7 preflight crew press conference transcripts, courtesy of NASA Historical Archives. Reprinted by permission.

Paul Robeson: Photo courtesy of CORBIS/Sean Sexton Collection.

Jackie Robinson: Photo courtesy of AP/Wide World Photos. Excerpt from *I Never Had It Made: An Autobiography* by Jackie Robinson as told to Alfred Duckett. © 1995 by Rachel Robinson. Reprinted by permission of the Ecco Press.

Fred Rogers: Photo © 1991 Gene Pushkar and courtesy of Family Communications, Inc. Excerpt © 1999 Family Communications, Inc. Reprinted by permission.

Franklin D. Roosevelt: Photo courtesy of CORBIS.

Jonas Salk: Photo courtesy of Culver Pictures, Inc./SuperStock. Excerpt republished with permission of Columbia University Press, 562 W. 113th St., New York, NY 10025. *Anatomy of Reality: Merging of Intuition and Reason* (extract), Jonas Salk, 1983. Reproduced by permission of the publisher via Copyright Clearance Center, Inc.

Benjamin Spock: Photo courtesy of CORBIS/Bettmann. Excerpt reprinted from *A Better World for Our Children* by Benjamin Spock, M.D. Used with permission of NTC/Contemporary Publishing Group, Inc.

Gloria Steinem: Photo © 1999 Jenny Warburg. Excerpt © 1997 by Gloria Steinem. Reprinted by permission of Gloria Steinem. The entire version of this article originally appeared in the September/October 1997 issue of *Ms*.

Jody Williams: Photo © Kitchener-Waterloo Record, 1998. Excerpt © 1999 by Jody Williams. Reprinted by permission.

Babe Didrikson Zaharias: Photo and text courtesy of Gray Library, Special Collections, Lamar University. Reprinted by permission.

NEW WORLD LIBRARY

publishes books and cassettes that inspire and challenge
us to improve the quality of our lives and the world.

Our books and tapes are available
in bookstores everywhere.
For a free catalog of our complete library
of fine books and tapes, contact:

New World Library
14 Pamaron Way
Novato, CA 94949

Phone: (415) 884-2100
Fax: (415) 884-2199
Or call toll free: (800) 972-6657
Catalog request: Ext. 50
Ordering: Ext. 52

Email: escort@nwlib.com
Website: http://www.nwlib.com